ROYAL HISTORICAL SOCIETY
STUDIES IN HISTORY
SERIES
No. 27

THE PILGRIMAGE OF GRACE IN THE LAKE COUNTIES, 1536-7

Recent volumes published in this series include

For a complete list of the series please see pp. 159-60

THE PILGRIMAGE OF GRACE IN THE LAKE COUNTIES, 1536-7

Scott Michael Harrison

LONDON
ROYAL HISTORICAL SOCIETY
1981

DA
339
.H3
1981

The Society records its gratitude to the following, whose generosity made possible the initiation of this series: The British Academy; The Pilgrim Trust; The Twenty-Seven Foundation; The United States Embassy bicentennial funds; The Wolfson Trust; several private donors.

The publication of this volume has been assisted by a further grant from The Twenty-Seven Foundation.

Printed in England
by Swift Printers (Sales) Ltd
London E.C.1.

CONTENTS

MAPS AND TABLES

MAPS

TABLES

PREFACE

The thesis upon which this study is based was presented for the degree of Master of Letters at the University of Lancaster in 1975. It was the product of one year of full-time and three years of part-time research. I am indebted to a number of people who contributed directly or indirectly towards its completion.

The thesis itself was directed and encouraged by Dr. A.L. Beier, and any postgraduate student would be lucky to have a supervisor so diligent and long-suffering as he has been throughout the course of my work. To the staff of the Joint Archive at Kendal and Carlisle I owe my introduction to and mastery of the more difficult sources which I encountered in this study. My examiners, Professor A.H. Woolrych and Dr. C.S.L. Davies, having awarded my degree, gave me further encouragement and advice concerning errors or misjudgements which would have to be cleared up in preparation of the work for publication. Professor G.R. Elton kindly pointed out many of the practical failings of my initial presentation, and suggested considerable restructuring of the book which I have since attempted to effect. Dr. C. Haigh pointed out some errors which had escaped my notice to the very end, and made some final suggestions for improvements. Mr. R. Newns kindly redrew my maps.

'To my family, for their encouragement and forbearance, I owe the greatest debt.'

Scott Harrison

LIST OF ABBREVIATIONS

A.H.R.	*Agricultural History Review*
BL	British Library
CWAAS.	*Transactions of the Cumberland and Westmorland Archaeological and Antiquarian Society.*
E.H.R.	*English Historical Review.*
Ec.H.R.	*Economic History Review.*
LP	*Letters and Papers, Foreign and Domestic, of the Reign of Henry VIII,* ed. J.S. Brewer, J. Gairdner, R.H. Brodie (1862-1932).
L.C.R.S.	Lancashire and Cheshire Record Society.
PRO	Public Record Office.
Valor	*Valor Ecclesiasticus Tempore Henrici Octavus Institutus.*
V.C.H.	*Victoria County History.*

INTRODUCTION

The Pilgrimage of Grace of 1536-7 is generally agreed to have been the greatest and most dangerous of the Tudor rebellions. For a short time King Henry VIII lost control of the whole of the north of England, and civil war seemed a likely prospect.

The importance of the rebellion to Tudor history is indicated by the great amount of attention paid to it by historians. It is not only the subject matter which has made the study of the Pilgrimage of Grace so attractive, but also the historiographical controversy which surrounds almost every aspect of the events of those months. Since the publication of the major work on the Pilgrimage of Grace by Madeleine and Ruth Dodds in 1915 few new facts have been discovered about the events of the rebellion.[1] However, a considerable number of studies have appeared which examine the events of 1536-7 from different interpretative viewpoints, resulting in the prolonged debate which is still by no means resolved.

Several recent contributions to the understanding of the rebellion have taken the form of regional or local studies. M.E. James and M. Bowker examined the rebellion in Lincolnshire,[2] R.B. Smith that in the West Riding of Yorkshire,[3] and D.M. Palliser the situation in York itself.[4] C. Haigh has provided the only detailed examination of the contribution of a north-west county, Lancashire,[5] although M.E. James in his articles on two men of power in the Lake Counties made some tentative statements concerning the rising there.[6] Surveys of the historiography of the Pilgrimage of Grace have demanded more of this local and regional information before satisfactory answers to the

[1] M.H. & R. Dodds, *The Pilgrimage of Grace and the Exeter Conspiracy*

[2] M.E. James, 'Obedience and Dissent in Henrician England: The Lincolnshire Rebellion, 1536', *Past and Present*, No. 48 (1970),and M. Bowker, 'Lincolnshire 1536: Heresy, Schism or Religious Discontent' in D.Baker (ed), *Studies in Church History 9. (1972).*

[3] R.B. Smith, *Land and Politics in the England of Henry VIII: The West Riding of Yorkshire, 1530-46.*

[4] D.H. Palliser, *The Reformation in York, 1534-53*, University of York, Borthwick Papers, No. 40 (1971).

[5] C. Haigh, *The Last Days of the Lancashire Monasteries and the Pilgrimage of Grace*, Chetham Society, third series, Vol. XVII (Manchester, 1969).

[6] M.E. James, *Change and Continuity in the Tudor North. The Rise of Thomas, First Lord Wharton*, University of York, Borthwick Papers, No. 27 (1965); 'The First Earl of Cumberland and the Decline of Northern Feudalism', *Northern History*, I, 1966.

problems of the rebellion can be given.[7] The object of this study is to provide information on one such area, the Lake Counties.

The Pilgrimage of Grace in the Lake Counties has generally been seen as a movement composed of a poverty-stricken rabble whose base economic motives lowered the tone of a northern rising which at least pretended to have its roots in the defence of the old religion. The Dodds sisters wrote that the rebellion in the north-west was essentially 'a rising of the poor against the rich' in which 'the commons showed no zeal for the church and treated the clergy with little respect'. As such 'the mass of eager but undisciplined commons were as great an anxiety to the leaders of the rebellion as they could be to their opponents'.[8] This view largely complies with that of R.H. Tawney, who suggested that 'having heard mass . . . with the blessing of the vicar [they went] on a crusade to put an end to gentlemen and withheld rents and fines'.[9] Rachel Reid, the first historian to suggest that the Pilgrimage of Grace was an overwhelmingly secular and economic rebellion, used documents relating to the Lake Counties as the backbone for her thesis.[10] Since the publication of *The King's Council in the North* in 1921 several criticisms have been made of Mrs Reid's interpretations of the rebellion as a whole, although the view of the part played by the Lake Counties remains unchallenged. A.G. Dickens, for example, has said of the rising there 'that it is agreed to have been a social and economic affair, little related to any aspect of the Reformation'.[11] Slightly more caution was used by C.S.L. Davies in saying that, in the Lake Counties and Craven 'economic aims figured more prominently than elsewhere'[12] a view echoed by R.B. Smith in his recent study of the West Riding of Yorkshire.[13] Messrs. C.M.L. Bouch and G.P. Jones stand almost alone in saying that other non-economic grievances were present in the minds of the rebels of the Lake Counties, and that the clergy there played a more important role than has generally been credited to them.[14]

[7]C.S.L. Davies, 'The Pilgrimage of Grace Reconsidered', *Past and Present*, No. 41 (1968).

[8]Dodds, Vol. 1, p. 225.

[9]R.H. Tawney, *The Agrarian Problem in the Sixteenth Century*, p. 319.

[10]R. Reid, *The King's Council in the North*, pp. 123-60.

[11]A.G. Dickens, *The English Reformation*, p. 178, an idea echoed in A.G. Dickens, 'Secular and Religious Motivation in the Pilgrimage of Grace', in G.J. Cuming (ed.), *Studies in Church History* 4 (1967).

[12]Davies, 'Pilgrimage of Grace Reconsidered', p. 55.

[13]Smith, *Land and Politics*, p. 204.

[14]C.M.L. Bouch and G.P. Jones, *An Economic and Social History of the Lake Counties, 1500-1830*, p. 41.

This study means to show that all of these assessments of the rebellion in the Lake Counties fall short of the whole truth. The Pilgrimage of Grace there was far more complex in origin and in action than previous writers have alleged. Of primary importance in the continuing debate is the problem of motivation, and the first sections will examine the background to the rising and the question of rebel grievances. An analysis of the rebellion itself will provide answers to other significant questions: what was the composition of the rebel crowd, and how was it led and organised; was there any connection between the rebellion in the Lake Counties and that in adjoining regions; and more broadly, what do the answers to these questions suggest about the importance of the Pilgrimage of Grace within the context of Tudor history?

Primary sources for the study have not been abundant, and on occasion it has been necessary to admit that the limitations of the evidence allow only tentative conclusions to be made. The most copious source is the great body of material calendared in the *Letters and Papers, Foreign and Domestic, of the Reign of Henry VIII.*[15] Only occasionally have I found that the calendar has missed or misinterpreted a piece of important evidence, and in all cases where I have quoted from the original letter rather than the calendar I have stated the full manuscript reference.[16] Spellings have normally been modernised. Another valuable set of sources has been the records of Star Chamber, Chancery, and the Duchy of Lancaster courts, which provide a vast amount of material on all aspects of law and order in the region.[17] Other useful sources in the central record collections include estimates of population, commissions and depositions relating to such things as enclosure disputes, tenant right and tithes, and surveys and rentals of estates in the Lake Counties.[18] Unfortunately, the latter relate largely to the reign of Elizabeth I and after, but they occasionally provide useful pieces of information. One other small but valuable find lay among the Sheriffs' Accounts which provided some details of the goods and chattels, and hence some idea of the social background, of rebels executed in Cumberland.[19] Family estate documents are thinly scattered, and I have found no good series to use

[15]Ed. J.S. Brewer, J. Gairdner, R.H. Brodie (23 vols. in 38; London, 1862-1932). Hereafter *LP*.

[16]Hereafter PRO, S.P.I.

[17]Hereafter PRO, STAC.2; PRO, C.1; PRO, D.L.I.

[18]Population estimates in BL, MS Harley 594, and PRO, Chantry Returns. Full references are given for Rentals and Surveys, Commissions and Depositions in the appropriate places.

[19]PRO, E. 199, 7/41.

for a thorough examination of economic trends in the region. Percy records at Carlisle, Dacre records at Durham, and Clifford records at Kendal and Chatsworth have been invaluable, but only because of the relative scarcity of anything else.[20]

In total, it has been necessary to treat the sources with caution. The confessions of rebels are subjective and often demonstrate little more than an attempt to avoid retribution. The accusations of loyalists sometimes appear to be clouded by personal feelings, or to be ill-informed. Court proceedings are inevitably one-sided and rarely objective. Tax returns for the region do not exist; population estimates such as chantry returns provide only wild approximations; and estate documents are too few to form any clear picture of how the policies of the owners were changing.

Accepting these failings, much valuable material still remains which allows the historian to make an assessment of the Pilgrimage of Grace in the Lake Counties. It is hoped that this in turn will contribute to our knowledge of the rebellion as a whole and its importance in Tudor history.

---

[20]The Joint Archives Committee for the Counties of Cumberland and Westmorland, and City of Carlisle (hereafter Joint Archives, Carlisle, or Joint Archives, Kendal); Durham, The Department of Palaeography and Diplomatic; and Chatsworth, Manuscripts of his Grace, the Duke of Devonshire.

1

THE POVERTY OF THE LAKE COUNTIES

The Lake Counties of the sixteenth century formed a region inclined towards poverty rather than wealth, dearth rather than abundance. Westmorland, for example, was a rugged and barren county containing fewer people for its size than any other county. This poverty can be attributed to two factors: firstly, the subjection of the region to constant raids from Scotland; secondly, over-population due to the inability of the region's natural resources to sustain its inhabitants.

Incursions from Scotland had sporadic economic effects. Economic development was inhibited by the perpetual insecurity of the borders, and little industry or accumulation was encouraged by the lawlessness of the region. Threats of destruction also created the need for the maintenance of a defensive border force. Even the smallest tenants of the Lake Counties often held their lands by tenure akin to knight's service.[1] The performance of their duties included the compulsory defence of the border at their own expense. War with Scotland, even if victorious, could thus make serious inroads into the precarious economic balance of the Lake Counties.

It has been stated that, for its size, the county of Westmorland had few inhabitants. This does not contradict the fact that the habitable areas of the region were severely overpopulated in the sixteenth century. The most reliable source of population statistics is an estimate of numbers of households in parishes within the Diocese of Carlisle compiled in 1563.[2] The survey has been used to construct an approximate total for the population in that year, calculating on a basis of four and one half persons to each household.[3] By this estimate Cumberland contained 45,786 inhabitants and Westmorland 27,564. In 1500 the total would have been less than the combined figure of 73,332 for the two counties in 1563, but for the purposes of this study the populations of North Lancashire and some Yorkshire parishes such as Dent and Sedbergh would have to be added. Any estimate of the population of the Lake Counties in 1536 is thus an approximation, and no statistics exist to show whether the population was growing. If it is accepted that the region was experiencing the same

[1] See below, pp. 66-7
[2] BL MS Harley 594.
[3] Bouch and Jones, p. 16.

expansion of population as other parts of the country, it had possibly grown by as much as ten per cent in the decade before the Pilgrimage of Grace.[4] The effect of such a rate of growth on a region which, as shall be shown, was already experiencing population pressure would have been serious.

More important than the total population is its distribution as indicated by the survey of 1563. The towns were not extensive and the county towns were not prospering. In 1563 Carlisle contained 450 households, and between 1535 and 1543 Leland wrote of the city that 'the whole site of the town is sore changed. For whereas the streets were great edifices, now be vacant and garden plots'.[5] Of Appleby, Leland commented that 'now it is but a poor village'.[6] In 1515 it was said to be 'greatly diminished and fallen into ruin', and according to the survey of 1563 it contained 227 households.[7] The only 'good market town' which Leland reported was Kendal. No reliable population estimate exists for the town, although six thousand 'housling people' were said to occupy the parish of Kirkby Kendal in 1545.[8] The chantry returns, from which this figure is taken, appear to be sweeping approximations for the Lake Counties, and it is uncertain which of the fifty or more villages and hamlets making up the parish were included. The other towns of the region were small, and even the old market towns such as Brough, Cockermouth and Kirkby Stephen may have been active only once a week. It is probable that less than ten per cent of the total population of the region lived in towns and that the remainder were dispersed in the rural parishes.

It may be significant that some of the most populous of the towns were deeply involved in the Pilgrimage of Grace. In Westmorland, Kirkby Stephen contained 300 households, Wharton 284, Morland 260, Orton 211, and Brough 140.[9] In Cumberland, Dalston contained 200 households, Caldbeck 182, and Penrith 140. The active Yorkshire parishes were also very populous, Sedbergh containing 663 households, of which 346 were in Sedbergh itself, 251 in Dentdale, and 66 in Garsdale. Of the 101 parishes for which data exist in

[4]J. Cornwall, 'English Population in the Early Sixteenth Century', *Ec.H.R.*, 2nd ser., 23 (1970), 43-4, suggests a growth in population from 2.3 millions in 1522-5 to 2.8 millions in 1545.

[5]J. Leland, *The Itinerary of John Leland in or about the Years 1535-43*, ed. L.T. Smith, V, 53.

[6]*Ibid.*, p. 47.

[7]BL, MS Harley 594. Bouch and Jones, p. 24

[8]PRO, E.301/11.

[9]BL, MS Harley 594.

Cumberland and Westmorland, thirty-two contained more than one hundred families, and thirty-eight contained les than fifty, the smallest being Kirkandrews and Rockcliffe with eleven and fourteen households respectively. These figures may be compared with others for Kent, where parishes contained from thirty to sixty households, or from one hundred to two hundred in thickly settled areas.[10] The average for parishes in the Lake Counties is eighty-five. This figure is statistically misleading, for some parishes in the region are vast, and certainly much larger than those in Kent.[11] For example, Crosthwaite contained 320 but in consequence of the size of the parish only twenty inhabitants could be found to the square mile. However, what the statistics do not show is that much of Crosthwaite, and of other parishes in the Lake Counties, was unfit for settlement. Thus it was remarked of Westmorland in 1622 that 'the smallness, barrenness, and the multitude of inhabitants in the habitable places of the county is such and so far incomparable to other counties of the Kingdom'.[12]

The great density of population in the Lakeland region has been attributed to the fact that there was plenty of meadow and pasture there, at a time when such land was in short supply in other parts of the country; and to the fact that many areas used a custom of gavelkind inheritance, which reinforced clannish family ties and encouraged all children to stay. Even where subdivision of estates was not practised, a second son could make an intake into the waste in order to provide himself with a small amount of arable land. Reclamation in this fashion took place in the sixteenth century in such places as Scotby, Inglewood and Skelton.[13] However, there were limits to the extent to which either subdivision could take place or intakes be made. By 1574 Grasmere was scattered into wretched parcels left after generations of subdivision.[14] Other townships, such as Brough, strongly resisted further intakes into the swiftly diminishing good pasture land.[15] The problem was created by the coexistence of, on one hand, a vast amount of open land which anyone could use, and on the other an acute shortage of good arable and meadow.

This shortage was more acute in some parts of the region than

[10]J. Thirsk, 'Industries in the Countryside', in F.J. Fisher (ed.), *Essays in Social and Economic History of Tudor and Stuart England* (1961), p. 82.

[11]C. Haigh, *Reformation and Resistance*, p. 22 deals with the size of parishes in Lancashire, which average 33 square miles compared with an average of 4 square miles in the Midlands and South East.

[12]A Statement made by the Westmorland Justices, quoted by Thirsk, p. 82.

[13]PRO, E.134, 13 Eliz.Hil.2.

[14]W. Farrer, *Records Relating to the Barony of Kendal*, ed. J.F. Curwen, II, 14n.

[15]*LP*, XII(1), 687(2).

others. For the purposes of this brief economic study, four types of land may be identified. Of these the best known is the Cumbrian Dome, the high land within a fifteen mile radius of High Raise. Most of the land there lies at more than seven hundred feet above sea level, and the lake-bound valley floors leave little space for human habitation. The great beauty of the region cannot hide the fact that the Cumbrian Dome is inhospitable to man, and settlement there was not encouraged until local industry, especially tourism, was established. Akin in type to the Lakeland fells are those of the Pennines, which reach across into Cumbria from Yorkshire. There, too, only the valley floors were suitable for occupation in the sixteenth century.

The lowlands of the region were therefore the main centres of population, and these consisted of the three remaining land types: the relatively fertile belt of land on the coast of Cumberland and north Lancashire and the mosses of the Solway estuary; the hill country to the south of Kendal, including Kirkby Lonsdale and adjoining Yorkshire parishes; and the Eden Valley. With the exception of the mosses, which deteriorate as they leave Carlisle to the north-east and which until modern times were poorly drained, the lowland areas were fertile and clement enough to encourage the establishment of communities. In such areas as the Eden Valley, the Cumberland coastal plain, and in Kendal where one could find 'little green hills flourishing with corn and grass', population may have been uniformly distributed, but this was not so in other areas.[16] Good land, even relatively level land, was so scattered and rare that any site offering some usable land was likely to be attractive for permanent settlement as the population density increased. In the marginal and upland zones of the region, 'a traveller in Tudor times would have seen small villages and hamlets, each surrounded by a few fields of cultivated land, with commons adjoining, and then a waste, stretching for miles until the next oasis was reached'.[17]

The paradoxical land shortage of the Lake Counties was not only reflected in the distribution of population. The agricultural systems of the region were designed to provide the optimum amount of good grazing land and the highest possible yield of grain. Despite this, neither was sufficient in quantity, and when coupled with rising population the result was a natural tendency towards food shortage.

Both climate and soil militated against corn growing. Climatically the highlands were particularly unsuitable, being ecologically subarctic in the character of their climate. Rainfall at Seathwaite is above

[16]Celia Fiennes, *The Journeys of Celia Fiennes,* ed. Christopher Morris, p. 190.
[17]Bouch and Jones, p. 17.

one hundred inches annually, hardly an encouragement to crop-growers. Elsewhere, the climate is not so extreme. The coastal area is vulnerable to westerly rain-bearing winds, but the Eden Valley is something of a rain shadow, the relatively small amount of thirty inches falling there each year. However, for the region as a whole the lack of sunshine and heavy rainfall discourage corn growing and favour grass.

The nature of the soil is also unfavourable to grain. The mountain zone has thin stony soil, or peat bogs unsuited to cultivation. Otherwise, much of the land is rock and scree. Even in lowland areas, little of the land is suitable for arable farming. In many areas heavy blue clay, dry and cracked in summer and waterlogged in winter, can be found. Peat formations on the clay have caused high acidity and worsened the soil. The Penrith ridge, on the other hand, is composed of light sands, heavily eroded and infertile. Only drumlins and pockets of boulder clay, or deposits of alluvial soil such as those at the head of Wastwater can be said positively to encourage tillage.

Climate, soil, and the short growing season also dictated the crop. Only on the Cumberland plain and in Furness was wheat grown. Elsewhere, the concentration was on oats, barley, and rye. Despite attempts to maximise production of these crops, in general they appear to have been inadequate.

It has been shown that most communities were established at any site with a small amount of good land. The arable normally took the form of a number of closes adjoining the houses of a community, or of an open field. There were few open fields in the mountains, or the moss and fell townships. There, the pattern of settlement tended to consist of isolated hamlets and dispersed farmsteads. Only nucleated villages sustained open fields. However, the open fields were still expanding in 1500, and of 288 townships in Cumberland it has been calculated that some 220 operated open fields.[18] Methods of utilisation varied considerably from parish to parish. In some places, a strict division was made between infield and outfield. The infield was annually manured and cropped, and the outfield cropped until exhausted, then used for pasture. More often, only one part of the open field would be cropped in a given year, working on a rotation basis. A system of five years cropping followed by five years fallow was common, although at Holm Cultram a nine year cycle was used.[19] One third of the land was cropped for three years, then rested for six

[18]G. Elliot, 'The System of Cultivation and Evidence of Enclosure in the Cumberland Open Fields in the Sixteenth Century,' *CWAAS,* new ser. 59 (1959), 89.

[19]F. Grainger, 'Agriculture in Cumberland in Ancient Times', *CWAAS,* new ser. 9 (1909), 125.

years, and rent and tithe were only paid on land which was under the plough. The open fields were also used for grazing. The practice of throwing open the fields to cattle after harvest appears to have been universal. In some places, summer grazing on the rheins (grass strips within the infield) was also practised, these areas being fenced off for the purpose. However, in all cases the amount of summer or winter grazing was inadequate, and stinting ensured that the slaughter of the bulk of the herd occurred each autumn.

The relationship in quantity of open field to private closes is uncertain. In all probability most landholders had a share in the open field separated from neighbouring strips by a permanent balk, and also a small close. This was the situation at Wasdale, where the total average holding was from three to ten acres. Similarly, at Aspatria tenants had closes varying in sizes from half a rood to an acre, plus holdings ranging from four to ten acres in the infield, and from two to four acres in the outfield. There were, of course, variations in size of holding according to status within the peasantry. As freeholders, copyholders and tenants at will all had shares in the common land, these variations could be considerable. The average size of yeomen's holdings at Kendal between 1605 and 1638 was twenty-four acres. In the absence of a wealthy yeoman class, few peasants' holdings were likely to be larger than this, while many were much smaller. An order made at Holm Cultram in 1538 stipulated that a man holding from fifteen to twenty acres of land should be prepared to serve on the borders with arms and mount, while at the bottom of the scale, a man with from two to six acres need only act as a footman with bow or spear. Undoubtedly footmen were in the majority throughout the region. Few farmers were fortunate enough to have twelve acres of land to cultivate. Even if one assumes that the customary acre in the Lake Counties is equal to three statute acres, holdings there were pitifully small. In Norfolk, where farmers tilled some of the richest land in England, the average size of holdings in 1549 was ten acres of land and the grain yield was far higher.[20] In Cumberland and Westmorland peasants tilled only enough to subsist, a mighty task in itself. For the region as a whole, it follows that the harvest was inadequate to feed the population even in years of plenty. Years of dearth were particularly damaging to the economy of the Lake Counties and exacerbated the normal state of poverty.

The most profitable branch of agriculture in the region was the breeding of cattle, both for dairying and for sale to lowland farmers, and the raising of sheep for their wool.

[20]Thirsk, p. 81.

The most important dairying and stockbreeding areas were in Dent, Sedbergh and the Eden Valley. These localities shared with all other parts of the region the problem of winter grazing. In summer common pasture was unlimited, and Aspatria was one of a small number of places in which stinting operated. However, the onset of winter saw transhumance to the sheltered lowlands, and usually the good grazing land was on the common field. At its worst, the shortage of lowland grazing called for the annual autumn slaughter of all but the essential cattle needed for domestic purposes. This ensured that neither dairying nor stockbreeding provided for much more than the demand from within the region.

Far more important to the economy of the Lake Counties was the breeding of sheep for wool. Despite the fact that it was 'the worst wool within the realm', and that the ewes were not very prolific, the production of 'Manchester cottons', 'Northern dozens', and 'Kendals' was the only major activity which brought trade and wealth to the otherwise impoverished region. The woollen industry was centred on Kendal, and throughout the surrounding area wool was worked on a domestic basis. Many households supplemented their income by carding, spinning, dyeing or weaving. Fulling mills were established on sites which could utilise the fast flowing streams of Lakeland, eighteen being found in the parish of Grasmere in the sixteenth century. Some areas specialised in particular facets of the trade. Dent and Sedbergh, for example, were deeply involved in the hand-knitting of stockings, the profits from which helped to supplement incomes hard-hit by the custom of gavelkind inheritance.

From the place of manufacture, woollen goods were transported to various parts of the country, and the green cloth of Kendal appears to have achieved a certain fame. One well-established trading connection was between Kendal and Southampton, between which chapmen regularly plied in the early sixteenth century. In 1536 fifty-three packs were carried to Southampton, which represented a good year for trade.[21] In return, items such as fruit, dyes, alum, wool flocks and canvas were transported to Westmorland. The woollen trade expanded throughout the sixteenth century, before entering a decline. Undoubtedly many people benefited from the trade, and much needed currency was brought into the otherwise economically isolated region.

Other than the profits of pastoralism and associated industry, there was little productive activity of more than local significance.

[21]W. Rollinson, *A History of Man in the Lake District,* p. 98, and B.C. Jones, 'Westmorland Packhorse men in Southampton', *CWAAS,* new ser. 59 (1959).

The exploitation of mineral resources did not reach an important dimension until after 1564, the date of the formation of the Company of Mines Royal. Before that time iron from Egremont, coal from Workington, lead from Alston, and a little silver were mined, but activity was sporadic and small scale.

Several minor industries were associated with the common wastes and woodlands. Stone and slate were quarried, mainly to serve local needs. The woodland industries were ancient, and at Hawkshead in 1537 profit was made from matting, making barrels, drying bark, and making frames for pack horses. However, charcoal burning was the most important woodland industry, and its importance increased in proportion to iron mining. Charcoal manufacture was later to cause concern as it made severe inroads into the woodland in places such as Furness, but this was not a problem in 1536.[22]

The coast also offered scope for small scale industry. Fishing and salt panning were both practised in a small way. The Cumberland and Lancashire coasts had some small ports, including Whitehaven and the Peel of Fouldray (or Peel), and Westmorland had the minor port of Milnthorpe. However, in 1566 only fifteen 'pickards' varying in size from seven to ten tons served the whole coast.

The isolation of the Lake Counties was increased by a lack of good roads. For the few travellers who did venture into the region houses of hospitality were few. Robert Aske, when defending the monasteries during the Pilgrimage of Grace, explained how the abbeys served 'strangers and baggers of corn as betwixt Yorkshire, Lancashire, Kendal, Westmorland and the Bishopric for there was neither carriage of corn and merchandise but was greatly succoured both horse and man by the said abbeys'.[23]

However, the quantity of intercourse between the Lake Counties and adjoining regions was small, only wool being a major export and corn a major import.

In total, the economic picture was a gloomy one. In normal times the inhabitants may have had difficulty in ekeing out their limited resources, and often turned to raids against the Scots or to riots against any tangible scapegoat for their economic problems. The deprivation of the region at the best of times undermined the forces of

[22]Bouch and Jones, pp. 26-8, and J. Thirsk (ed.), *The Agrarian History of England and Wales,* vol. IV Chapter 1, 'The Northern Province', pp. 16-27.

[23]*LP,* XII(1), 901. Aske's full statement is printed in M. Bateson, 'The Pilgrimage of Grace and Aske's Examination', *E.H.R.* (1890).

law and order in the Lake Counties. It will be shown that both 1535-6 and 1536-7 were years of dearth.[24] Consecutive bad harvests made it inevitable that the increased poverty of the region should promote large scale disturbances amongst the peasantry on economic grounds alone.

[24]See below, pp. 89-90.

2

THE STATE OF THE CHURCH IN THE LAKE COUNTIES

Few hard facts exist to indicate the state of the church in the Lake Counties before the Pilgrimage of Grace. The rebellion itself can tell us more about the attitudes and beliefs of the inhabitants of the region, for it was only at such time that people saw good reason to state them. The only evidence which does exist relates to the condition of the clergy in the years before the rebellion.

Contemporary anti-clerical opinion saw the clergy suffering from a general malaise which was reflected in ignorance and poverty on the one hand, corruption and pluralism on the other. Recent study has shown that such opinions had less foundation than has generally been supposed. In the diocese of Lincoln, for example, clerical offences were relatively low in number.[1] For the nation as a whole 'the men who did serve in the parishes, men perhaps of limited education and narrow capacities, were no doubt vulnerable to temptation, but chronic and universal indiscipline was not the result'.[2]

The north, perhaps more than any other region, suffered from clergy who were poor and ignorant, and Archbishop Lee of York wrote that 'many benefices be so exile [poor], of £4, £5, £6, that no learned man will take them, and therefore we be fain to take such as be presented, so they be honest of conversation and can competently understand that they read and minister the Sacraments and Sacre-mentals, observing the due form and right. . . . And in all my Diocese I do not know secular priests that can preach, any number necessary for such a Diocese truly not XII, and they that have the best benefices be not here resident.'[3]

How far did the benefices of the Lake Counties fit Archbishop Lee's description? Some of them certainly did, and two of the poorest were held by prominent members of the secular clergy in the Pilgrimage of Grace.[4] Sometimes such poverty appears to have driven the holders of benefices to breaches of the law. In 1532 John Ireby of Aspatria refused to give the last sacrament to Janet Brayton

[1]M. Bowker, *The Secular Clergy in the Diocese of Lincoln, 1495-1520,* Chapter III.

[2]P. Heath, *The English Parish Clergy on the Eve of the Reformation,* p. 188.

[3]H. Ellis, *Original Letters Illustrative of English History,* series 3, ii, p. 338.

[4]See below, pp. 102-3.

as she could not pay, and she died without confession.[5] In an undated case in the court of Chancery during Audley's Chancellorship (1532-44) the vicar of Isell, one Richard Dalton, a 'corrupte and covetouse man from whom the church had been granted away', broke down the church door and stole the offerings.[6] However, the Lake Counties in general seem on average to have had wealthier benefices than some other dioceses, possibly a product of the larger size of parishes there[7]. Of eighty-nine parishes relevant to this study, some forty-seven were rectories and forty-two vicarages, about the same ratio as in the dioceses of Lincoln and York.[8] The values of these benefices may be compared with those of the dioceses of Coventry and Lichfield and of Lincoln.

Table 1: Comparative values of benefices in the Lake Counties, the diocese of Lichfield, and the diocese of Lincoln.

	Under £20	Under £15	Under £10	Under £5
Lichfield	87%	79%	60%	10%
Lincoln	89%	80%	51%	6%
Lake Counties	76%	54%	39%	7%

[8a]The Lichfield figures were calculated by P. Heath for A.G. Dickens, and are quoted in Dickens, *English Reformation* p. 77. Figures for Lincoln are based on the calculations of gross income in Bowker, p. 140. Figures for the Lake Counties, including parishes in Cumberland, Westmorland, Lancashire and Yorkshire, are taken from *Valor Ecclesiasticus Tempore Henrici Octavi Institutus*, edited by Caley and Hunter, 5 volumes (London, 1825), Volume V, pp.259-60, 265-8, 272, 283-92, 294-8.

In the Lake Counties the average value of rectories was £8 15s. 8d., and that of vicarages £14 5s. 2d. These apparently high averages do conceal the fact that the poorest rectory was worth only £3 11s. 8d., and the poorest vicarage £4 10s. 2d. Furthermore it can be assumed that the parishes with the highest incomes were snapped up, and that

[5]PRO, C.I. 819.19.

[6]*Ibid.*, C.I. 758.38.

[7]Haigh, *Reformation and Resistance*, p. 22, has shown that this was also the case in Lancashire. Large parishes with growing populations were producing high incomes for incumbents.

[8]Dickens, *English Reformation*, p. 75. The ratio of rectories to vicarages in Lincoln was 317 to 311, and in York 392 to 230.

more of the rectories which remained in circulation were poor by national standards. Nevertheless the benefices of the region seem to have been better endowed than might be supposed from Archbishop Lee's remarks concerning the north in general.

Lee also commented that the most valuable benefices were often held by absentees. Some absenteeism was no doubt legitimate, as for example where priests had been appointed to responsible office outside their own parish. Others, however, appear to have held more than one benefice for purely financial reasons, or to have taken the fruits of benefices without thought for the concomitant obligations.[9] In the Lake Counties several priests held more than one benefice. These included Parson Threlkeld of Melmerby who held the vicarages of Lazonby and Dufton; Christopher Slee, Prior of Carlisle, who held that of Sowerby; John Clifton, rector of Clifton, who held that of Bromfield; John Graystock, who held the school at Brough as well as the vicarage of Warcop; John Herryng, rector of the college of Kirkoswald and Dacre, who held the vicarage of Crosthwaite; and Barnard Towneley, Chancellor to the Bishop of Carlisle, who was also rector of Caldbeck.[10] Many other vicarages of the region were appropriated to distant monasteries and were held by absentees who may also have been pluralists. The quality of the secular clergy in the region must have suffered as a result. It seems unlikely that the curates who deputised for absentees were of a very high standard. Certainly the curates at Kirkby Stephen and Kendal were held in little respect by their congregations, as was shown at the outbreak of the Pilgrimage of Grace, and they may have been typical.[11] Neither did the region gain from contact with the monasteries to which the benefices were appropriated as most of them were far distant, such as St Mary's at York.[12]

Archbishops Lee's statement must therefore be seen to have some relevance for the Lake Counties. Poor benefices were unlikely to attract clergy of high quality. Others which were on average 'less exile' than many northern parishes attracted pluralists who were often absent, so that the relative wealth of some benefices militated against the quality of religious service there.

Despite evidence that some parishes corresponded with Lee's

[9] Several cases of pluralism in Lancashire are described in Haigh, *Reformation and Resistance*, p. 26.

[10] *Valor*, V. 284-95.

[11] See below, p. 91. Haigh, *Reformation and Resistance*, p. 28 suggests that the traditional association of curates with neglect may have been overstressed.

[12] Heath, p. 81.

pessimistic estimate and were poorly provided for, it seems likely that in others the church was in a healthy state. In negative terms, the lack of any damning evidence of ignorance or crime amongst the parish clergy is an indication of this. A more positive demonstration of enthusiasm for religion at parish level is the quantity of church building which took place between 1500 and 1536, and this must to some extent reflect the performance of the clergy. Rebuilding, often on an extensive scale, occurred at Keswick, Beetham, Burton, Morland, Newbiggin, Ormside and Orton. New aisles were added at Kendal, Hawkshead and Kirkby Ireleth. New chapels were added at Kirkby Lonsdale and Heversham. Towers were added at Kirkby Stephen, Brough and Crosby Ravensworth, and the church at Ulverston was completely rebuilt. The religious zeal which is reflected by this activity indicates that parish life on the eve of the Reformation was very strong in the Lake Counties.

The monasteries provide rather more evidence for the historian. In relation to the size of the Lake Counties the monasteries were few in number and not particularly wealthy. North Lancashire could boast the Cistercian house at Furness, the richest in the county with an annual income of £946 1s. 10d., but neither the Augustinian Priory at Cartmel nor that at Conishead had an income of more than £125.[13] Cumberland contained the Cistercian Abbey of Holm Cultram, worth annually £535 3s. 7½d., and the Augustinian Priory at Carlisle, worth £482 8s. 1d., but the six other institutions were all very small, and only the Augustinian Priory at Lanercost, worth £79 19s. 0d., was mentioned in the context of the Pilgrimage of Grace.[14] Westmorland contained only one abbey, the Praemonstratensian institution at Shap. This was worth only £166 10s. 6½d. which made the county the poorest of the counties for which monastic income has been analysed.[15] Cumberland was twenty-seventh on a list of thirty-two, and Lancashire was twenty-second. In other words the monasteries appear to have reflected the general poverty of the area in which they were located.

However, monastic income is only an indication of size and influence and tells little of the spiritual condition of the institutions. This too appears to have been very poor, and the history of misconduct and neglect which surrounds the main institutions could

---

[13] *Valor,* V, 269-72. A full account of the condition of the Lancashire Monasteries appears in Haigh, *Lancashire Monasteries,* Chapters I and II.

[14] *Ibid.,* pp. 275-6, 282-3.

[15] *Ibid.,* p. 293. The analysis of monastic income is in A. Savine, *English Monasteries on the Eve of the Dissolution,* p. 98.

not have encouraged much loyalty in the rebels at the time of the Pilgrimage of Grace. The main evidence of moral misconduct comes from the questionable testimony of the visitors to the monasteries, Richard Layton and Thomas Legh, the latter of whom gained considerably in rewards of monastic land after the dissolution. Their findings are tabulated in Table 2.

Table 2: Cases of sodomy and incontinence in the monasteries of the Lake Counties as alleged by Layton and Legh.

	Numbers accused of incontinence	Numbers accused of sodomy
Furness	4, including the abbot.	1
Cartmel	2, one having six children.	—
Conishead	5, one with six, another with ten women.	—
Calder	2	5
Seaton	2, including the prioress.	—
St. Bees	—	2
Holm Cultram	8, including the abbot.	5
Lanercost	—	2
Wetherall	—	2
Lamplugh	3	—
Carlisle	3, including the prior.	7
Shap	—	—
Armathwaite	—	—
Total:	29	24

Source: LP, X, 364.

While the accusations of the commissioners have often been seen as exaggerations, there must have been some foundation for both the quantity and detail of cases cited above. Other evidence also exists which testifies to extremely disreputable incidents at the larger houses in the years immediately preceding the Pilgrimage of Grace. In September 1532 Gawyn Borrowdale, a monk at Holm Cultram, was implicated in the murder of Abbot Deveis by a justice of the peace, Sir John Lamplugh.[16] Borrowdale was put into custody pending an investigation. Poisoning was suspected but because the evidence was circumstantial no action was taken until the following year. In 1533

[16]*LP,* V, 1317, and VI, 1557.

the commissioner, Thomas Legh, wrote to Cromwell in defence of Borrowdale, saying that 'he is kept out of his house by malice and wrong information sent to you'.[17] At the same time the accused wrote to Cromwell requesting permission to go to London to protest his innocence. A re-appraisal of the circumstances of the murder was undertaken, and the evidence submitted was inconclusive. Borrowdale was said to have threatened that, if Deveis was elected to the office of Abbot, he would not last for a full year. Later, he was said to have stood at the cook's right hand during supper on the night before the Abbot became ill. Borrowdale's acquittal was no doubt logical in the face of such sparse evidence, but it is notable that in the aftermath of the Pilgrimage of Grace he became Abbot of Holm Cultram. His main function in that office was to hand over the monastery to the commissioners for the suppression, after which he was rewarded with the first rectorship of Holm Cultram. The connection between Borrowdale, Legh and Cromwell need hardly be stressed. Not only did Borrowdale use his influence to avoid the consequences of the murder trial, but he also managed to turn the situation to his own advantage and gain a valuable new position.

The Prior of Conishead was also accused of murder. On this occasion, in September 1533, Thomas Legh took the role of prosecutor.[18] A local gentleman, John Bardesey of Furness, whose father, William, was involved in several bitter disputes during the 1530s, was assaulted by several persons.[19] 'His head was cut asunder in three places and his leg in four places and his arms in three places and also smitten to the heart a great and deadly wound.' Legh accused the Prior of arranging the murder, but he appears to have been acquitted for lack of evidence. Prior Lord continued in office, and he too was involved in the scramble for land after the dissolution.

The most notorious institution in the Lake Counties was the Abbey of Furness. The evidence relating to the condition of the abbey has been thoroughly examined elsewhere, but the essential details are worth reconsideration here.[20] Perhaps the greatest charge made against the Abbot, Alexander Banke, was yet another accusation of murder. A quarrel took place within the abbey over office-holding, and it was stated that Banke had attempted to arrange the murder of

[17]*Ibid.*, VI, 985. Other correspondence relevant to this case can be found in VI, 986 and 988.

[18]*Ibid.*, VI, 1124.

[19]PRO, S.P.I, vol. 79. p. 64. (*LP*, VI, 1124)

[20]Haigh, *Lancashire Monasteries* Chapter I, and *Reformation and Resistance*, pp. 83-4.

his opponent. The murder did in fact take place after the charge was made, but the Abbot obtained a pardon. It was remarked at the time that the acquittal was brought about by influence rather than innocence.[21] Banke was certainly a notorious figure, being involved in many incidents which brought the monastery into disfavour before his death in 1531. His first misdemeanours in the period after 1509 were concerned with estate policy. In that year, he attempted to reduce his customary tenants to something approaching servile status. In 1516 he was taken to the Duchy of Lancaster court by a tenant, William Caase, on the charge that he had evicted the tenants of the village of Selergarth.[22] This village was turned to pasture, causing the decay of thirteen ploughs. The following years saw the continuation of such disputes between the Abbot and his tenants and neighbours, tithes and tolls often being the issues in contention.[23] Banke's legacy must have been one of hatred and disaffection towards the monastery which his successor cannot have found easy to overcome. Indeed the new Abbot, Roger Pyle, found many obstacles in the way to improving the general condition of Furness Abbey. Before his appointment the keys to the abbey chamber were entrusted to one Hugh Brown who stole some property from the chamber, broke open the abbey chest, and forged documents using the abbey seal. After his appointment trouble with the monks continued, for Pyle was forced to report in August 1533 that three of them 'cannot be contented to obey me'.[24] The ringleader of the three was imprisoned and later dispatched to the Isle of Man. Trouble with tenants also continued after 1531, for Pyle seems to have pursued the estate policies of Alexander Banke. In 1534 Pyle accused several 'riotous persons' of pulling down his hedges and driving away his sheep. In a comprehensive reply Leonard Braithwaite, a tenant of the abbey, claimed that he had been refused entry to his rightful inheritance, which should have been permitted by tenant right on payment of a heavy entry fine of £6 13s. 4d.[25] Instead, the Abbot had turned the property over to pasture, and when Braithwaite attacked the enclosure, three hundred sheep were found to be grazing there. The Abbot also attempted to undermine the traditional perquisites of tenant right. John, Robert and Nicholas Fisher were accused of felling oak trees in Furness. They defended themselves by referring to custom, saying that the felling of

---

[21]*LP,* VI, 1124.

[22]PRO, D.L.I, vol. II, C.3.

[23]PRO, STAC.2, 19/129; 898/27; D.L.I, vol. VIII,R.6.

[24]*LP,* VI, 787.

[25]PRO, D.L.9, F.1.

trees was permitted when houses became in need of repair.[26] They further compounded their alleged crime by disrupting the Abbot's court which, they said, would not give their case a fair hearing. In total, the larger houses of the Lake Counties appear to have been in a poor condition, and the largest, Furness, alienated its tenants by the pursuit of modernising estate policies.

There were, of course, many aspects of monastic life which brought benefits to the community. Despite the failings of the monasteries it is possible that the services which they provided engendered loyalty towards them. Robert Aske, one of the most prominent of the leaders of the Pilgrimage of Grace, gave several reasons why the monasteries should be preserved, and three of them seem to be applicable to the Lake Counties.[27] Aske suggested that 'by the occasion of the said suppression the divine service of God is much diminished'. Until the aftermath of the Pilgrimage of Grace, when Furness provided the government with the key to total dissolution, only the smaller institutions (that is, those worth less than £200) were threatened. Therefore the Lake Counties were liable to lose nine out of their twelve institutions in 1536, although one of these, Shap, was for the time being exempted.[28] The spiritual function of the monastery is an intangible. However, Aske's general comment on the fact that 'divers and many of the abbeys were in mountains and desert places, where the people be rude of conditions and not well taught the law of God' does seem particularly applicable to the Lake Counties which stood to lose not only the threatened institutions but also the valuable supply of parochial priests.[29] By the loss of the monasteries an already poor area can only have become poorer, both spiritually and materially.

Aske's second defence was founded on the statement that the 'abbeys in the North parts gave great alms to poor men and laudably served God'. It has been calculated that the national average of alms was equal to 2½ per cent of gross income.[30] As has already been shown elsewhere the Lancashire monasteries were generous by comparison.[31] Furness gave compulsory alms totalling 4.8 per cent of gross income, including the keeping of thirteen paupers and eight widows. Conishead gave eight per cent in alms, and Cartmel 10.7 per cent,

[26]*Ibid.*, STAC.2, 15/278-80.

[27]*LP,* XII (1), 901, M. Bateson, 'Aske's Examination', *E.H.R.* (1890).

[28]*Ibid.*, XI, 1217(14).

[29]Haigh, *Reformation and Resistance,* p. 122.

[30]Savine, p. 239.

[31]Haigh, *Lancashire Monasteries,* p. 54.

including daily doles for seven poor men.[32] The institutions of Cumberland and Westmorland were rather less generous. At Holm Cultram £3 was distributed to the poor on Maundy Thursday, and £7 was allocated amongst five paupers.[33] This totalled a meagre 1.2 per cent of gross income, which the abbey attempted to raise to 1.9 per cent by claiming as alms a fixed annual payment of £5 6s. 2d. towards the maintenance of sea defences on the Cumberland coast. The Augustinian Priory of Carlisle gave 4.5 per cent of its gross income away in alms, but not all of this benefited the poor.[34] Amongst the costs which were included was that of maintaining a wax light in memory of Gilbert Weeton, a Bishop of Carlisle, and twenty shillings spent annually in paying for masses for the souls of Edward IV and his wife. Wetheral was not conspicuous for its almsgiving, providing £2 13s. 4d. for the benefit of paupers, a mere 2.1 per cent of its gross income.[35] Of the Cumberland monasteries, only Seaton was generous according to the statistics, giving 7.2 per cent of its income in alms.[36] However, this amounted to only £1 of its income of £13 17s. 4d. Shap, the only monastic institution in Westmorland, made a moderate payment of 3.5 per cent of its gross income to paupers on Good Friday and Maundy Thursday.[37]

The *Valor Ecclesiasticus* does not, of course, show anything other than compulsory alms and those allowed by the commissioners to be free of the royal tenth. Other services were provided for the community by the monasteries. The Abbey of Furness was responsible for draining and reclaiming lands on the Lancashire coast, and for maintaining sea defences, a service which was also performed at Holm Cultram. Also there was a custom at Furness by which tenants who paid their rents in kind received gifts including beer, bread, dung and iron. Similarly at Holm Cultram, when tenants performed boon days, they had 'great commodity and benefit from them'.

In total, it may be said that the monastic institutions of Lancashire justified Aske's faith in their role as almsgivers. Their neighbours in Cumberland and Westmorland were less generous, but most of them compared favourably with the national average. Even the lowly 1.9 per cent of gross income given out by Holm Cultram was no disgrace

[32]*Valor*, V, 272.

[33]*Ibid.*, pp. 282-3.

[34]*Ibid.*, pp. 275-6.

[35]*Ibid.*, p. 10.

[36]*Ibid.*, p. 265.

[37]*Ibid.*, p. 293.

in comparison with the 1.7 per cent of much richer institutions such as Fountains Abbey in Yorkshire.

Aske also suggested that travellers were 'well succoured by the abbeys'. He made particular reference to the need for places of hospitality for 'strangers and baggers of corn betwixt Yorkshire, Lancashire, Westmorland and the Bishopric'. Travellers as well as local people would suffer from the loss of these facilities.

Aske's other justifications of monastic life are less relevant. The institutions of the Lake Counties do not seem to have been great centres of learning. Although a schoolmaster had certainly taught boarders at Furness at some time before the dissolution, one of the accusations against the abbey after the rebellion concerned the fact that the monastery had not kept a schoolmaster.[38] Aske also remarked upon the fact that the monasteries kept 'all gentlemen much succoured in their needs with money'. This has been attributed to the practice of fee allocation to local gentlemen who acted as stewards, bailiffs and seneschals, which hardly seems a worthy motive for defending the monasteries. More important, such fees as were granted by the institutions of the Lake Counties did little to earn the support of gentlemen at the time of the Pilgrimage of Grace, but rather whetted their appetite for land at the time of the dissolution.[39]

It seems unlikely that Aske's arguments for the defence of the monasteries would have outweighed their notorious reputations in the minds of the people of the Lake Counties. Therefore it might be expected that monks who called on the people of the Lake Counties to help them defend their monasteries would receive an unenthusiastic response. If, too, numbers of the secular clergy were unexceptional or absent, little in the way of a major role could be expected of clerics in the Pilgrimage of Grace. Even so, it has been shown that there were priests who were maintaining thriving parishes, and some of these were willing to lead the pilgrims in rebellion. Elsewhere the lack of clerical leadership was to be compensated for by the laity, and this may be the greatest indication that the church in the Lake Counties was still playing a strong and meaningful part in the lives of ordinary people.

---

[38]*LP*, XII(1), 841(2), Bouch and Jones, p. 29.

[39]Bouch and Jones, pp. 55-6. Amongst those people in the scramble for monastic land were Lord Dacre, Sir Thomas Wharton, and Lord Monteagle.

3

THE STRUGGLE FOR POWER IN THE LAKE COUNTIES

A recent study of the Pilgrimage of Grace has suggested that a significant correlation exists between the areas which rose up in rebellion and the commitment of the lords and gentlemen dominant there.[1] Where a Percy or a Darcy threw in his lot with the rebels, so did his tenants. Where a lord remained loyal to the King, his tenants were restrained. Such a hypothesis is not applicable to the Lake Counties because of the equivocal attitude of the gentlemen there, who were neither involved in the leadership of the Pilgrimage of Grace nor in a position to take any concerted action to promote the King's law.[2] The result was that, while the rebels had no traditional feudal leader, any restraining influence was also absent. To discover why men of power and influence in the region were neutral and impotent during the months of rebellion it is necessary to examine the course of events in the politics of the Lake Counties in the preceding years.

At the centre of these events was a dispute between ruling families over the office which conferred upon its holder supremacy in the counties adjacent to the Scottish border — the office of Warden of the March. In time of peace the problem of the border with Scotland was so distant that the King and his ministers doubtless found it convenient to forget that such places existed.[3] However, in time of war or internal disturbance the northern marches were of vital strategic importance. On each of the western, middle and eastern marches a strong warden was needed whose main duties were to defend the northern counties and to organise and lead offensive raids into hostile territory. In time of peace it was his duty to organise regular meetings with his Scottish counterpart at which grievances could be redressed and thus goodwill maintained.[4]

Of necessity the office of warden brought with it many advantages for the holder. Perhaps most important, the warden was given military

[1]Smith, *Land and Politics,* Chapter 5.

[2]See below, pp. 79-85.

[3]For an illustration of the application of this idea to an earlier period, see P. McNiven, 'Rebellion and Disaffection in the North of England 1403-8', unpublished M.A. thesis, University of Manchester, 1967, p. 2.

[4]For a thorough account of the duties of the warden, see D.L.W. Tough, *The Last Years of a Frontier. A History of the Borders during the Reign of Elizabeth.*

command of all available forces within the border region. The office also carried a considerable salary and influence in the appointment of officers to royal stewardships within the region. In the Lake Counties these included the castles of Carlisle, Penrith and Bewcastle, and several royal manors such as Scotby and Inglewood. All these stewardships were vitally important if the warden was to have dominance of the region within his authority.

The appointment of warden presented a difficult choice to the King. In order to ensure the strength of the border, a considerable amount of power had to be vested in one man or group of men. By making an individual strong the King created a second potential problem — an overmighty subject who could use his control of the north as a threat to the throne itself.[5] One possible solution was to select a loyal man who could be placed above the heads of the traditional ruling families of the north, but experiment had shown that a stranger who did not have the support of local families was rendered impotent in the execution of his office. Therefore selection had to be made from the existing men of power within the march. Where only one candidate was present, the enhancement of that man's power was a risk that the King had to take. Where there was more than one candidate, the choice of one man at the expense of rival groups could lead to intense rivalry and subsequent deterioration in the effectiveness of the office.

In the western march there were two suitable candidates for the office of warden. The Nevilles and Percys, so dominant in the fifteenth century, had since been eclipsed by the rival houses of Clifford and Dacre. The possession of the wardenship had become the new centre of a dispute which had long raged between the two families, and the continuing dispute was to have great significance for the political situation at the time of the Pilgrimage of Grace.

The Cliffords had first acquired lands in Westmorland in 1299 when Robert, first Lord Clifford, inherited a moiety of the Vipont lands in the Barony of Westmorland.[6] In 1310 the castle at Skipton and considerable estates in the West Riding of Yorkshire were gained by exchange, and henceforth Skipton became the centre of Clifford influence. The other moiety of the Vipont lands was inherited in 1344 and completed Clifford domination of the Barony of Westmorland. The control of powerful castles at Brough, Appleby and Brougham, and the hereditary retention of the office of sheriff of Westmorland,

[5] See R.L. Storey, *The End of the House of Lancaster,* Chapter VII.

[6] B. Burke, *Dormant, Abeyant, Forfeited, and Extinct Peerages of the British Empire,* pp. 122-4.

firmly established the importance of Clifford influence in the Lake Counties. However, the Cliffords were not elevated to the status of Earls of Cumberland until 1525. The family had supported the house of Lancaster in the Wars of the Roses, and the young Henry Clifford had been educated at the court of Henry VII with the young Henry Tudor. A friendship was established which bore fruit for the Cliffords in royal favours, of which the Earldom was perhaps the greatest. In terms of wealth the Earl of Cumberland was at least equal to neighbouring lords. In the subsidy of 1536 he was assessed at £33 6s. 8d., in comparison with the Earl of Northumberland's £25.[7] In terms of power the Clifford influence was paramount amongst the upper and middling gentry of the Lake Counties. Tied to the Cliffords by landholding, friendship or self interest were Sir John Lowther, Sir Thomas Curwen, Sir Robert Bellingham and Sir William Musgrave, to name but the most powerful.[8] Furthermore, before 1536 the Earl could rely on the support of Sir Thomas Wharton of Wharton in Westmorland.[9] It has been mentioned that the power of the Percy family in the north west had declined since the fifteenth century. Percy landholding in Cumberland was still considerable, but the influence derived from it appears not to have rested with the Earl of Northumberland, but with Sir Thomas Wharton who was the comptroller of the Percy estates, and who as an enemy of the Dacres naturally gravitated towards their rivals, the Cliffords. However, as Percy influence declined and Wharton looked for a new source of patronage he turned away from local lords and towards the King. By 1536 he was becoming a potential rival of both the Cliffords and the Dacres, and indeed he replaced them as the King's representative on the western march in 1537.[10] Even so, before this time he must be counted as sympathetic to the Clifford interest, if not from patronage, at least because of his rivalry with the Dacres.

The Dacres came from humbler origins than the Cliffords, although their roots in the history of the Lake Counties went deeper.[11] In 1248 a Dacre first became Sheriff of Cumberland, despite having modest means as a basis for influence. In 1317 the Dacres increased their resources when Gilsland was gained by marriage. The heiress to whom the Gilsland estates had descended was abducted from the Cliffords. During the Wars of the Roses the Dacres were at first

[7]*LP*, Vol. XI, 139.

[8]James, 'First Earl of Cumberland', pp. 50-1.

[9]See James, *Change and Continuity,* for a thorough study of Wharton's career.

[10]M.L Bush, 'The Problem of the Far North: a Study of the Crisis of 1537 and its Consequences', *Northern History* 6 (1971), examines this situation in depth.

[11]*Burke's Peerage,* pp. 152-3.

Lancastrian, Ranulph Dacre falling at Towton, but later their allegiance was switched to the Yorkists under Edward IV. At that time Sir Humphrey Dacre was elevated to the title of Lord Dacre of the North. Despite their uncertain loyalties, the family continued to fare well in the reign of Henry VII. In 1487 a second heiress was abducted from the Cliffords and brought with her the Greystoke estates, which doubled Humphrey Lord Dacre's landholding. At the expense of further alienation from the Cliffords, the Dacres had acquired a strategically vital block of land which completed a formidable and compact section of the border.[12] Dacre power increased with the appointment of Thomas Lord Dacre to the wardenship of all three marches in 1511.[13] This monopoly of power represented rather a lack of any more suitable candidate than a reflection of Dacre's particular talents, and his wardenship in the east failed through lack of local support. Thomas was succeeded by his son, William Lord Dacre, in 1525.[14] With the assistance of his uncle, Sir Christopher Dacre, William maintained a dominance of the Western March until 1534. However, in terms of wealth and influence the Dacres were apparently no match for the Cliffords. Dacre support was confined to the lower gentry in the Lake Counties, although beyond the region they were tied by marriage to the Earl of Shrewsbury, Lord Scrope, and Lord Conyers. Closer to home the Dacres had to rely on smaller families such as the Threlkelds, Leghs, and Lancasters.

There can be little doubt that there was a vast difference between the respective qualities of wardenship of Clifford and Dacre. This was largely a product of the contrasting situations of the two factions, and the fact that anything which benefited Dacre was directly disadvantageous to the Cliffords.

Lord Dacre's greatest advantage lay in his control of the vast and compact block of land adjacent to the border itself. Moreover, Dacre had retained the vestiges of feudalism on these estates in order to maintain an effective military force, both for offensive and defensive purposes. Dacre's lands received the brunt of any Scottish attack, and his tenants had to be prepared to defend their own lands. Moreover, raiding could be far more profitable than scraping together a meagre living on the infertile border mosses. The Dacre tenants, being weaned on war, gained a reputation for military strength which made them a considerable force for any enemy to reckon with. In the light of this, one can assume that there could not be a weak Dacre, for a strong

[12] See Map 1 (p. 29 for areas of territorial influence.

[13] *LP*, I,984

[14] *Ibid.*, IV, 1779.

man was needed to hold these tenants in check. Thomas Lord Dacre, William Lord Dacre, and Sir Christopher Dacre were all respected by their tenants, and their service on the border demonstrates their military capabilities.[15] The Dacres also realised the necessity of maintaining their strength, even at the expense of ignoring the temptations of land exploitation which were becoming the rule elsewhere. In 1536 William Lord Dacre ordered a reform of estate policy, but not a reform which would sacrifice the loyalty of his military tenancy.[16] If, for example, a tenement was unoccupied, he ordered that his officers give preferential treatment to an archer who could serve him in the event of disturbances on the border by demanding a lower entry fine than would otherwise be expected. Dacre thus maintained the advantages of solidarity of estates, loyalty of tenants, and military ability. All these advantages militated against the Cliffords, whose disposition was entirely different.

Whereas the Dacres were educated to the facts of living on the border, the Earl of Cumberland had been raised at court and had developed no particular military ability. As a result of this, instead of the characteristics of the feudal magnate, Clifford had developed the life-style and habits of a courtier and landowner. It is apparent that the Earl not only failed to provide the leadership which was required in the Lake Counties on the eve of the Pilgrimage of Grace, but also tended to undermine his own position by exploiting and alienating his tenantry. Adequate proof of this fact can be found from evidence relating to the enclosure riots in Craven in 1535. The Earl's tenants in Giggleswick were involved in pulling down his enclosures, and despite the fact that rioting occurred near the Clifford stronghold at Skipton Castle, the Earl himself showed no particular zeal in restoring law and order.[17] Further dissatisfaction amongst the Clifford tenants was to manifest itself during the Pilgrimage of Grace, for he was unpopular not only for enclosing land but also for raising rents and fines and for attempting to exploit ancient military tenures.[18]

The Earl of Cumberland's estate policies were also a possible cause of disaffection amongst the gentlemen who traditionally served the Cliffords. The mesne tenants, from whom much of Clifford power stemmed, were being exploited in the same way as the lesser tenants on the Earl of Cumberland's estates. Rents for knights' fees which had

---

[15] The significance of this point is dealt with below, pp. 82-3.

[16] Durham, Department of Palaeography and Diplomatic, C/201/9.

[17] *LP*, VIII, 863, 893, 946.

[18] See below, pp. 54-6, 63-5.

Map 1

Landholding and Territorial influence in the Lake Counties

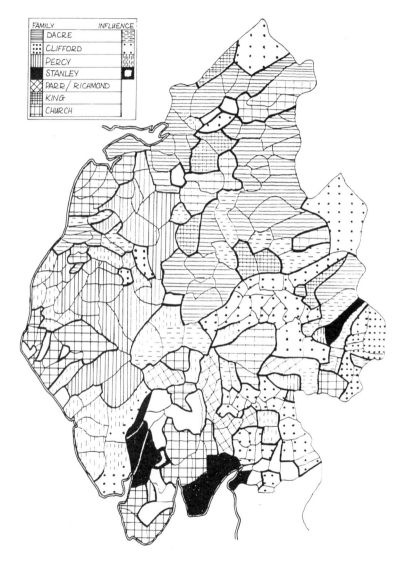

FAMILY	INFLUENCE
DACRE	
CLIFFORD	
PERCY	
STANLEY	
PARR / RICHMOND	
KING	
CHURCH	

been stable at £27 9s. 7d. for many years were raised to £42 4s. 7d. soon after 1526.[19]

Perhaps for these reasons, it was Dacre rather than Clifford influence which was predominant on the Western March in the early sixteenth century. Thomas Lord Dacre had been warden until his death in 1525. At this time the wardenship reverted to the Earl of Cumberland, but in the face of deteriorating relations with Scotland the Earl's inadequacy for the task was revealed. In December 1527 William Lord Dacre was appointed as warden, and in consequence the rivalry between the families of Clifford and Dacre and their respective supporters began to intensify.

Between December 1527 and September 1529 the main cause of disputes between Clifford and Dacre was the control of lands around Carlisle which was normally associated with the wardenship. In 1525 the governorship and the stewardship of surrounding estates had been transferred to the Earl of Cumberland. Perhaps as a palliative to the Earl, he did not lose these offices when the wardenship reverted to Lord Dacre in 1527. Dacre was intensely annoyed that all the traditional perquisites of the wardenship had not been granted to him, and he pursued a campaign, using all means within his power, to wrest the offices in contention from the Cliffords.

In June and September 1528 the Earl of Cumberland complained that Dacre was harrassing the King's tenants on the Carlisle estates by stealing their corn and imprisoning some of them at Naworth. On the latter occasion up to four hundred Dacre followers were allegedly involved.[20] Indictments against various Dacre tenants, some of whom were allegedly acting under instruction from William Lord Dacre, were preferred in October 1528, and charges varied from the theft of grain to assault on Clifford servants.[21] An order was made by the King to stop Dacre's interference with the lands in contention, but Dacre pleaded that he could not govern the March effectively if he was obstructed by the City of Carlisle. Dacre's persistence was eventually rewarded, for in August 1529 he was granted the governorship of Carlisle.[22] This concession was probably made by the King because of the worsening relations between England and Scotland. It was expedient to give way to Dacre's demand until the trouble had passed over.[23]

[19]James, 'The First Earl of Cumberland', p. 46.

[20]*LP*, IV, 4790.

[21]*Ibid*., 4419, 4420, 4790, 4835.

[22]*LP*, IV, 2374, 4495.

[23]*Ibid*., 4790.

Between 1532 and 1534 England was in dispute with Scotland, and during this time there were outbreaks of lawlessness instigated by both Dacre and Clifford. In 1532 some tenants at Orton, a Dacre enclave in Westmorland, were attacked by about thirty rioters led by Christopher Wharton, brother to Sir Thomas.[24] One Thomas Atkinson, the man responsible for Dacre's sheep in Orton, was severely beaten and his hay was thrown into the river. While it was not explicitly stated that the Cliffords were behind the attacks, they must have looked kindly on any challenges to Dacre authority in Westmorland. The moiety of Orton and the manors of Dufton, Yanwath, Brampton and Bolton had long been a thorn in the Cliffords' side.[25] Nominally the Earl of Cumberland was the owner of the estates, but the tenant was Lord Dacre, whose ancestors had acquired them long before the Cliffords had gained an interest in Westmorland. The tenure was by cornage which, being tantamount to freehold, gave Dacre the effective ownership of the land on payment of a sum which bore no relationship to the real value.[26]

Lord Dacre was also responsible for the initiation of attacks on Clifford servants at the time of the war with Scotland. Robert Briscow, who was one of the deputies to the Earl of Cumberland, was attacked at Hensingham in 1532 by rioters led by John Skelton, a Dacre servant.[27] On that occasion he was evicted from his property, but on a second date, unfortunately unknown, Thomas Dacre, an illegitimate son of Lord Dacre, led some two hundred people against Briscow to cut and take away the grass growing on his land.[28] Further riots and disturbances perpetrated by both Briscow and his enemies occurred in 1533.[29]

The war with Scotland ended in 1534. During the war Dacre had led raids into Teviotdale, but was accused by the Earl of Northumberland of negligence in allowing some of his prisoners to escape, as well as in allowing Bewcastle to be destroyed.[30] However, these charges alone are insufficient to explain why, within three days of the end of the war, William Lord Dacre and his uncle Sir Christopher were arraigned by the King to be tried in the court of the Lord High Steward

[24] PRO, STAC.2. Vol. II, 2/151. Incidents of lawlessness can be located on map 2, p. 43.

[25] Joint Archives, Carlisle, Survey of Clifford's Knight's Fees, 1526.

[26] See below, p. 64., for a continuation of this dispute.

[27] PRO. STAC.2, 6/96-7.

[28] *Ibid.*, 6/263.

[29] *Ibid.*, 6/370.

[30] *LP*, V, 1286, and VI, 199, 876.

on a charge of treason.[31]

There seem to be two reasons why Dacre was arrested at this time. Firstly, the end of the war provided the King with an opportunity to reassert himself on the border with Scotland. As long as strong leadership had been required to combat the Scots, Dacre had been indispensable. However, he had been wielding his authority with a heavy hand, as was demonstrated by this campaign to gain the stewardship of Carlisle, and with the war concluded the time was ripe for the King to pluck down an overmighty subject. Secondly, during the course of the war Dacre's chief supporter at the court had fallen from power, to be replaced by Thomas Cromwell. There can be little doubt that the bastion of Dacre authority had been Cardinal Wolsey who had sponsored Dacre nominees for office even against the candidates of the King. In 1517 Sir Christopher Dacre had gained the stewardship of Penrith in preference to the King's boyhood friend, Lord Henry Clifford.[32] In return for such favours, the Dacres reciprocated with support for Wolsey. One area in which they were of use to him was in the administration of his northern estates. At the time of a rent strike on Wolsey's lands in Hexham in 1515, Lord Dacre and Sir Christopher imprisoned the ringleaders and burned the houses of tenants who resisted.[33] On the death of Lord Dacre in 1525 his son William quickly went to London where he attended Wolsey at Hampton Court.[34] No doubt he hoped to inherit the support of Wolsey and the obvious benefits which would accrue from it.

No such goodwill could be expected from Thomas Cromwell. The new minister was not interested in sponsoring great lords who built up their own powers at the expense of the King. Instead, Cromwell looked for officers who were willing to put their monarch above themselves and to turn away from the traditional pattern of border clientage.[35] One such man was Sir William Musgrave, who appears to have been used by Cromwell in the attack on Lord Dacre. The enmity between Musgrave and the Dacres was well established. In 1520 Thomas Lord Dacre and Sir Christopher had ruled in favour of Margaret Musgrave, and against Sir William, in a Star Chamber adjudication.[36] In 1530 Dacre and Musgrave were adversaries in the

[31]*Ibid.*, VII, 962.

[32]*Ibid.*, II, 4541.

[33]*Ibid.*, 64, 158, 250.

[34]*Ibid.*, IV(1), 4234.

[35]James, 'The First Earl of Cumberland', p. 46. This thesis does not entirely agree with that of M.L. Bush, 'The Problem of the Far North', which does not see any pre-conceived policy of opposition to great magnates.

[36]PRO, STAC,2, 30/74.

same court, the latter having taken rents due to Dacre on the Bewcastle estates.[37] Musgrave was ordered to stop intercepting the rents, but despite this in 1534 he was again accused of taking Dacre's rents and fines to the value of £104 13s. 4d.[38] Relationships between the two were also strained on other fronts. In 1528 Dacre accused Sir William of releasing an important prisoner from Carlisle.[39] At the same time Dacre reported that he could do nothing with Bewcastle, the stewardship of which had recently been granted to him, as the Musgraves had taken away the lead, smashed the windows, and allowed the whole place to fall into great decay.

In 1534 Musgrave made several charges against Dacre.[40] Primarily he accused him of having 'sought traitorously to deceive the King', several instances being cited: that Dacre had machinated with the intent that Musgrave and his tenants might be slain by the Scots; that Dacre had made a private treaty with Thomas Armstrong, the head of a lawless clan which occupied the 'debateable land', for surety against acts of war committed by Armstrong in the western march, with the exception of Musgrave; that, seeking the destruction of the Earl of Northumberland, Dacre had made a treaty with Lord Buccleuch which excepted the Earl from a non-aggression pact; that a treaty had been made with Robert Lord Maxwell similarly excepting Sir William Musgrave; and that during the war Dacre would allow nothing to be done to the annoyance of the Scots. Specific raids made at Musgrave's expense and details of meetings between the Dacres and their Scottish counterparts were cited.

Despite all these charges, the case against Dacre was not very strong. Thomas Armstrong was no more than a border thief, and just as obnoxious to Scotland as to England. He illegally inhabited the 'debateable land', the no-man's land where the border was not firmly established. In 1526 Dacre was ambushed by three hundred Armstrongs, as he had not allowed them to settle on the debateable land.[41] In April 1528 Dacre raided Armstrong territory, burned houses, and executed two of the Armstrongs at Carlisle.[42] In 1531 Dacre tenants were involved in an affray at Bewcastle, but it is not clear whether they were merely keeping the peace, or whether they

[37]*Ibid.*, 19/127.
[38]*Ibid.*, 19/127.
[39]LP, IV, 4134.
[40]*Ibid.*, VII, 962.
[41]*Ibid.*, IV(1), 2374.
[42]*Ibid.*, 4134.

were intervening on the side of Armstrong or Musgrave.[43] The fact that they were accused of atrocities in the debateable land at this time indicates that they still had no sympathy with the Armstrongs.[44] Even had there been an alliance, it would not have been against the interests of Henry VIII. James V was also unhappy with the border thieves, and in 1530 he had executed six of their number.

The alleged alliance with Robert Lord Maxwell was more likely, but again not unhelpful to England. Maxwell was the head of the most powerful family of south-west Scotland, holding the Baronies of Caerlavrock and Granane with the stewardship of Annandale and Kirkcudbright.[45] Maxwell was sympathetic to Dacre, for in 1531 it was suggested secretly at the instigation of James V that Maxwell and Dacre should combine to clear the debateable land.[46] By 1544 Maxwell was under assurance to the English Crown and active on its behalf. Maxwell's only particular animosity seems to have been towards Musgrave, who was sent home by Dacre on the occasion of meetings with Maxwell, and who complained about Maxwell's behaviour in 1535.[47] Dacre's relationships with Lord Buccleuch seem even more clear-cut. In 1535 Buccleuch was arraigned for treason, being accused of complicity with Dacre in burning property in Scotland. Buccleuch was acquitted, and by implication, Dacre also.[48]

Thus most of the accusations against Dacre seem to have been fabricated by Musgrave. However, he was not strong enough to attack Dacre alone, and his accomplice was undoubtedly Cromwell.[49] After the arrest of the Dacres, Musgrave wrote to Cromwell:

> Touching the Lord Dacre and Sir Christopher his uncle, and therfore sir I pray you stand stiffly in this matter and that I may have your gentle aid, for divers of this country and especially those that is bound for the Lord Dacre goods to the King's Grace will in no wise trust that he shall have any overthrow ... but from they see he shall go down I doubt not but they will say crucify! for the country has been so overlaid with the Lord Dacres that they thought here was none other King.[50]

[43]*Ibid.*, V, 477.

[44]*Ibid.*, 535.

[45]T.I. Rae, *The Administration of the Scottish Frontier, 1513-60,* p. 26.

[46]*LP*, V, 1054.

[47]*Ibid.*, IX, 844.

[48]Rae, pp. 170-172.

[49]*LP*, VII, 962, and XV, 403.

[50]PRO, S.P.I, 84, p. 199 (*LP*, VII, 829).

The implications of the letter are twofold. Firstly, it is certain that Cromwell was conversant with the charges, and that Musgrave knew that Cromwell would support him. Otherwise he would surely never have sent a letter which could incriminate him. Secondly, Musgrave was acting independently of the Cliffords, although they were involved to the extent that they were 'bound for the Lord Dacre's goods'. That is to say that the Cliffords had been informed of the forthcoming arrest and had been entrusted with the task of searching Dacre property to look for incriminating evidence. However, the Earl of Cumberland was forced to report that despite his secrecy Sir Christopher Dacre had some forewarning of the arrest and that, because of this, nothing incriminating could be found against him.[51]

In the first instance the indictment was put on 15 June 1534 at Carlisle before a jury consisting almost entirely of Clifford clients and others, such as the Earls of Northumberland and Westmorland, who had little sympathy with the Dacre cause.[52] This jury found that there was a case to answer, and on 9 July 1534 Dacre was tried before a panel of peers at the Court of High Steward, Westminster on charges of treason.[53] He was unanimously acquitted, and the only incriminating evidence against him, for which he was temporarily returned to the Tower, was the authorship of two dubious but trivial letters. He was pardoned for these on the payment to the King of a fine of ten thousand pounds.[54]

Such an acquittal was uncommon in the reign of Henry VIII. As Eustace Chapuys, the imperial ambassador, remarked, 'no one ever knew a man to come to the point he has done and yet escape'.[55] Chapuys also correctly interpreted the reason for the acquittal when he wrote that 'the Duke of Norfolk and others could not dissemble about the said acquittal fearing that if Cromwell began to lay his hands on such blood, he would follow the Cardinal' to a position of great power.[56] Lord Darcy echoed this sentiment after the Pilgrimage of Grace when he accused Cromwell of working to be rid of noble men but that 'though thou wouldest procure all the noblemen's heads within the realm to be stricken off, yet shall there one head remain that shall strike off thy head'.[57]

[51]*LP*, VII, 676 and 679.

[52]*Ibid.*, 962.

[53]The comments of Eustace Chapuys on the trial are in *LP*, VII, 1013.

[54]*Ibid.*, 1270.

[55]*Ibid.*, 1013.

[56]*Ibid.*

[57]*Ibid.*, XII(1), 976.

Clearly, at the time of the Dacre trial Cromwell was seen to be behind the accusation of treason. This is more apparent when one considers general policies during the decade to reassert the King's influence on the borders of the realm at the expense of the great nobility. In 1537 the eastern march was effectively brought into the King's hands by the Earl of Northumberland's will, which made the King his heir.[58] Dacre was a stronger man than the Earl, and the concoction of a treason trial was the only satisfactory way to be rid of him. Musgrave, the initiator of the conspiracy, may be seen as a useful tool who stood to gain considerably by the downfall of his enemy. The Cliffords were powerful allies, undoubtedly sympathetic to any such plot. However, the plan would have had little prospect of success without the agreement of Cromwell. It may have been an unpleasant surprise and a minor setback to Cromwell's plans that Dacre escaped the plot, but the question of guilt or innocence was in fact immaterial in the sense that Dacre was broken either way. An overmighty subject was dismissed from office, and in his place, in September 1534, the Earl of Cumberland was made warden of the Western March.[59] Dacre law was overthrown, but unwittingly the government had substituted the only real alternative — no law at all.

Having been released from the Tower, Dacre returned to the north to attempt to reassemble the broken pieces of his wealth and power. More important, he appears to have returned with the determination to resist, either through non-cooperation or through positive action, the wardenship of the Earl of Cumberland. His first task was to reclaim the property which had been so quickly confiscated by the Earl and his associates in 1534. This included sheep to the value of £111 4s. 0d., gold and silver worth £518 9s. 1d., and plate worth £1397 14s. 0d.[60] These items were returned in 1535, but others held by the Cliffords, in particular sheep and lambs, tithe corn, entry fines and rents from the Dacre estates, remained in contention.[61] Furthermore Dacre found that some lead had been taken away from his property and stored at Appleby, a Clifford stronghold, presumably on the assumption that it would no longer be required. At the close of 1534, in July 1535, and in August 1536 Dacre made formal complaints to the King about the Earl's retention of his goods.[62] The Earl was ordered to return all sheep and wool, making payment

[58]J.M.W. Bean, *The Estates of the Percy Family, 1416-1537*, p. 153.

[59]*LP*, VII, 1014, 1217.

[60]Durham, Department of Palaeography and Diplomatic, C/201/3.

[61]*LP*, VII, 1549.

[62]*Ibid.*, and XI, 477.

for any sold or killed while in his possession. Furthermore a sum of £17 12s. 6d. was to be paid to Dacre for corn removed from his tithe barns, the lead was to be returned, and a silver flagon which the Earl of Cumberland had retained was also to be given back to Dacre. In return, Dacre had to pay a sum of £200 to the Earl, presumably for his expenses as custodian of Dacre's property.[63]

The Earl's failure to return these items became a source of violent dispute during 1535 and 1536. Dacre could get no redress at law, so he appears to have given his tenants a free hand to reclaim his property by any method which they cared to choose. In July 1535 the Earl of Westmorland, head of the Neville family, was sent to the Lake Counties in order to put down riots caused by Dacre tenants.[64] Sheep which were allegedly stolen at the time of the Dacre trial had been forcibly removed from Clifford lands, enclosures had been thrown down at Smardale, and when a servant of Sir Edward Musgrave (a Dacre client) was murdered, Dacre's tenants had turned out in force to mete out their own brand of justice on Sir Thomas Wharton, whose servants were suspected of the crime.[65] A further catalogue of crimes committed by Dacre tenants (undated but probably relating to 1535 and early in 1536) throws light on other unlawful incidents.[66] Tithe barns at Kirkland and Bolton which had been recently awarded to the Earl of Cumberland were raided, the corn being carried away to Kirkoswald castle. John Hunt, a surgeon and servant of the Earl of Cumberland was taken forcibly from Cotehill to Dacre by Lancelot Lancaster, a prominent Dacre man, who kept him there to face imprisonment and 'punishment' for three days. After the grant of the stewardship of the Abbey of Holm Cultram to Dacre, his tenants went to the monastery, broke open the door, and threw out the former steward and his goods. This man, Thomas Dalston, had held his office from the Earl of Cumberland. Finally, it was suggested that Dacre tenants had committed various robberies, sold horses to the Scots, and caused friction between the town and garrison of Carlisle.[67]

This violence by Dacre tenants was specifically intended to redress a personal grievance in terms of regaining confiscated goods. Undoubtedly, Dacre's resentment over this issue must have been dwarfed by his anger at losing the coveted wardenship and its

[63]*Ibid.*, VII, 1549.

[64]*Ibid.*, VIII, 1030.

[65]*Ibid.*, VIII, 1030, 1046.

[66]*Ibid.*, VIII, 310. The locations of these, and other crimes committed in the years preceding the rebellion, can be found on Plate B, p. 59.

[67]*Ibid.*, 1030.

perquisities. The arbitration between the rivals attempted to cushion the effects of this loss as far as Lord Dacre was concerned.[68] The Earl of Cumberland, was made governor of Carlisle, steward of the royal manors in Cumberland, and steward of all the manors and lordships of the Bishop of Carlisle, the Priors of Carlisle and Wetheral, and for a short time, of the Abbot of Holm Cultram. He also gained the leases of parsonages and tithes previously held by Dacre. However, certain rents and farms pertaining to the tithes, fees of stewardships, payments owed to Dacre for the period of his wardenship during 1534, and an annual payment of ten marks a year for the duration of the Earl's wardenship, were all made over to Dacre.[69] Even so, from the viewpoint of the Dacres the new situation was most unsatisfactory. Dacre considered himself to have been severely wronged by the Crown and the Cliffords, and he was quite willing and able to undermine the new wardenship in order to restore his power.

The hostility of the Dacres and the inadequacy of the Earl of Cumberland as warden of the march thus created a vacuum of power. Lawlessness was the inevitable consequence of such a situation, and it is evident that this lawlessness was intensified by the actions of the Earl of Cumberland himself. There can be little doubt that one contributory factor to the political crisis of 1536 was the prolonged attempt by the Earl to gain political and legal ascendancy in the Barony of Kendal.

It has been shown that the Earl's only estates in the Lake Counties lay in the Barony of Westmorland. Separating this land from the Clifford estates in Yorkshire was the southern part of Westmorland known as the Barony of Kendal. No particular individual dominated this area. Estates were held by several families including the Parrs, Layburns, Bellinghams, Stricklands and Lowthers. These last three were tied to the Cliffords, so that the Earl of Cumberland was able to exercise considerable influence in the Barony. However, Parr and Layburn controlled the area around Kendal itself, and they were the upholders of the legal interests of the Duke of Richmond, of whose jurisdiction the Barony was a part. Sir William Parr, an active royal servant, was largely absent from the Lake Counties, although his correspondence demonstrates a keen interest in the situation there.[70] The man who solely maintained the rights of Parr and the Duke of Richmond was the Steward of Kendal, Sir James Layburn, the

[68]*Ibid.*, VII, 1549.

[69]*Ibid.*

[70]*Ibid.*, V, 951.

controversial head of a modest gentry family whose lands were centred on Ashton and Carnforth. The Earl keenly resented this jurisdictional block to his power in Westmorland, and during the course of the 1530s he pursued a campaign against the individuals in Kendal who obstructed him. Effectively, the dispute was between the Earl of Cumberland and Sir James Layburn, but allies and tenants of both parties became deeply involved.

In 1530 a servant of Sir James Layburn, Christopher Godmond, was evicted from his estate of four messuages and one hundred and four acres of land by John Hodgson, bailiff to a Clifford man, Sir Robert Bellingham.[71] A complaint was taken to the Duke of Richmond's court, which periodically sat at Kendal. The court adjudged that the eviction by Bellingham's men was wrongful, and instructed that Godmond should be allowed to re-occupy his property, and be paid compensation during the interim period. In response Bellingham ignored the order of the court and compounded the offence by stealing some of Godmond's cattle.[72] The case was heard again, and the court once more ordered that property and cattle should be restored. A fine of £100 was threatened should the order be disobeyed. Godmond re-entered his lands, but as soon as Richmond's court had removed from the area nine oxen and five cows were stolen by Bellingham's servants who drove them into Yorkshire. At this stage, the case was transferred to the jurisdiction of the court of Star Chamber which upheld the ruling of the Kendal court and ordered Sir James Layburn to ensure its execution.

This case appears to have been one of the first in which a 'line-up' of contesting influences can be seen. Not only was the Richmond Barony of Kendal able to oppose the unlawful activities of a powerful client of the Earl of Cumberland, but also Sir James Layburn was the man considered most suitable to uphold the administration of good law there. Later cases clearly demonstrate the animosity which was borne against Layburn by the Clifford interest.

The feud continued in April 1532, when William Parr wrote to Thomas Cromwell complaining that one Robert Tarne, 'a very insolent person', had entered his park at Kendal on various occasions with the intention of stealing his game, and on one occasion Tarne had provoked the keeper, William Redmayne, into a fight.[73] When Tarne was injured, he threatened to 'trouble' Redmayne and sue Sir James

[71] PRO, STAC.2, 16/96-8.
[72] *Ibid.*.
[73] *LP*, V, 951.

Layburn. In his letter Parr stated that the Earl of Cumberland was maintaining Tarne 'for the malice they bear my cousin Laborne for my Lord of Richmond's and my causes'. He further wrote that whereas by ancient custom he and his ancestors had always administered justice in Kendal, these 'sundry wealthy and malicious persons' were now sending poor people who could not afford it to the courts in London.

Tarne's suit did not appear until 1534, by which time his circumstances had changed considerably. Tarne acused Layburn 'of his malicious purposed malice and evil will which he had long borne toward me' of commanding several men including William Redmayne to murder him near Kendal. The complainant stated that he was assaulted by eight persons who 'sore wounded and beat him by several wounds in his head and maimed him breaking his arm in several places'. Later, the assailants returned and cut off his ear. Tarne reversed William Parr's complaint by saying that a poor man such as he could get no redress at common law because 'the said Sir James is steward of Kendal and also of great power blood and ally in the said country'.[74]

Before the case was heard Layburn wrote to Cromwell, protesting his innocence and claiming that he was in London at the time of the incident.[75] His suggestion to Cromwell that 'evil will is surmised against me by such men' must have referred not only to Tarne, but also to the Cliffords. Effectively, Layburn and the Cliffords had identified each other as opponents in the struggle for the jurisdiction of Kendal, and the dispute became largely a personal one between them. In 1533, the Earl of Cumberland had trespassed on the jurisdiction of the customary authorities in Kendal. Layburn complained to the King, who directed instructions to the Earl 'commanding him to cease meddling with my Lord of Richmond's liberties'.[76] Despite this, interference continued, and Layburn reported that the Earl's officers 'ceasseth not to molest and grieve daily my said Lord of Richmond's inhabitants . . . as well in the taking of distresses as otherwise to the great loss of our men' living there. Layburn also pleaded that 'for doing of my said office I am daily in jeopardy of my life by the said Earl and his servants or other by his payment'.[77]

Between the time of the King's letter and the occasion of the Duke of Norfolk's visit to Kendal after the Pilgrimage of Grace, interference by the Earl of Cumberland continued, and on 1 April 1537 Layburn

[74]PRO, STAC.2, 30/105.

[75]PRO, S.P.I., 83, pp. 65-7. (*LP*, VII, 432).

[76]PRO, S.P.I., 75, p. 77 (*LP*, VI, 306).

[77]*Ibid.*.

wrote to Cromwell reporting offences committed by the Earl.

> The said Earl by colour that he is sheriff of the said county of
> Westmorland has of late days held and kept the sheriff turn
> within the said Lordship of Kendal, and distrained divers of the
> inhabitants and tenants of the said Lordship for fines and
> amercements set and affirmed in the said turn. Where in very
> deed the same Earl has no authority to keep any such turn within
> the same Lordship nor to compel the inhabitants to appear at the
> turn held within the said county.[78]

The Earl was further accused by Layburn of punishing offences
committed at fairs and markets and of wrongfully indicting Layburn
for punishing tenants who had infringed local customs.

It was fortunate for Layburn that Clifford was unable to pursue the
feud during the Pilgrimage of Grace, when revenge might have gone
unnoticed. In 1538 the problem at Kendal was still unsolved, for Sir
Roger Bellingham and Sir John Lowther attempted to hold the 'sheriff
turn' at Kendal until Layburn, backed by a force of men, reminded
them of the Duke of Norfolk's order and sent them away.[79]

For at least seven years, therefore, the Earl of Cumberland's
ambitions in the Kendal area were frustrated by a modest gentleman
who served the Duke of Richmond, and through him the King. Like
Sir Thomas Wharton, with whom he appears to have been on friendly
terms, Sir James Layburn was setting an example of the course which
should be taken in order to succeed under the rule of Henry VIII.[80]

The advantages of serving the King were not lost on some
gentlemen of the north-west,and during the years of the dispute at
Kendal the heads of other families drifted away from the Cliffords and
towards the King. These included Sir Richard Tempest of Bolling in
Yorkshire and Sir John Lowther of Lowther. The failures of the Earl
such as that at Kendal may have been instrumental in snapping the
feudal ties and losing the Cliffords their time-honoured support, which
in turn made the Earl even weaker.

The political situation in the Lake Counties was of crucial
importance in the months preceding the Pilgrimage of Grace and
explains much of what took place during the rebellion itself. After the
Dacre trial of 1534 rivalry between the two leading families brought
about a rising crescendo of open violence. Lord Dacre, by far the

---

[78]PRO. S.P.I., 88, p. 53. (*LP*, VI, 1620).

[79]*LP*. V, 966. This document appears to have been misdated, as the events described
must have occurred after the rebellion.

[80]Evidence of Wharton's favour towards Layburn can be seen in *LP*, XI, 666.

strongest figure in military terms, not only failed to give his support to the Earl of Cumberland in his capacity as warden of the March, but actively opposed him in order to gain revenge for his own political downfall. Without Dacre support any wardenship would have been rendered impotent, and the Earl was unable to maintain any semblance of law and order. This did not bode well for his capability to deal with any problem from the real enemy, the Scots. Worse than this, the Earl of Cumberland was actively contributing to lawlessness in his attempt to gain control of the Kendal area by illegal means. His failure to achieve his ambitions there because of the resistance of modest opposition undermined the little support which he did retain in the region as a whole.

Both Dacre and Clifford were contributing towards an atmosphere in which rebellious spirits thrived, and one was unwilling, the other unable, to keep the situation under control. A power vacuum was created which is of primary importance in explaining why, in October 1536, rebellion was able to take such a complete and unrestrained hold on the Lake Counties.

Map 2

Recorded incidents of lawlessness in the Lake Counties 1530-6.

4

REBEL GRIEVANCES

The Pilgrimage of Grace was in many ways a reactionary rebellion. Whether the motives of the participants are seen to rest primarily in the spheres of religion, politics, or economics, the rebels wanted to re-establish the traditions and practices which their fathers had known. For that reason, the origins of the Pilgrimage of Grace will be examined as grievances, and only in the study of the rebellion itself will the methods used by the rebels to redress those grievances be analysed.

The problem of weighting these grievances is considerable, and has been subject to much debate already. Generalisations about rebel complaints can only be made in negative terms: the Pilgrims of Grace were not united on a religious crusade; they were not bound together under a political faction which wanted to overthrow the King; they were not all suffering from the economic difficulties prevalent in the decade before the rebellion, and which may have been particularly biting in that year. The Pilgrimage of Grace was an umbrella which covered all these parts. As long as the movement was able to put forward an all-embracing manifesto of grievances with which any rebel could identify himself in part, the rebellion could hold itself together in an appearance of unity. A comprehensive manifesto could also conceal differences in social status, for it is likely that there was mutual distrust and even antagonism between nobility, gentlemen and commons within the rebel ranks. Certainly in the most important areas of the rebellion, the nobles and gentlemen monopolised the leadership, and the York Articles presented on 15 October 1536, express only their grievances. However, the Pontefract Articles, which were compiled before 2 December, are more representative of all areas of rebellion and all social groups, although there can be little doubt that the spirit of the York Articles remained.[1]

An analysis of the Pontefract Articles gives a clear statement of the grievances of the Pilgrims of Grace. A number of the complaints expressed there reflect the views of the men of the Lake Counties. Others are irrelevant to the north-west, and some of their grievances were not considered important enough to relay to the King's Council.

Several of the Pontefract articles concern religion, and perhaps their predominance and the subsequent crusading atmosphere of the

[1]*LP*,XI, 705 and 1246. The Pontefract Articles are printed fully in Fletcher, *Tudor Rebellions*, pp. 128-30.

rebellion can be attributed to the influence of the Yorkshire gentleman Robert Aske. A general and rather confused complaint was made against a broad spectrum of heretics whose works the rebels wished to be 'annulled and destroyed'. Heretic bishops were also the subject of complaint, the rebels wishing 'their sect to have condign punishment by fire or such other, or else to try their quarrel with us and our partakers in battle'. More specific was the demand that 'the abbeys suppressed to be restored unto their houses, land and goods'. The confession of Robert Aske clearly demonstrates the importance which he attached to the preservation of the monasteries. Partly his defence rested on the monasteries' spiritual function in serving God and teaching religion to the people. However, he also stressed the social and economic aspects of monastic life, such as relieving the poor, providing hospitality for travellers, and helping the sick and aged. Another clause of the articles asked that the payment by the religious houses of first fruits and tenths to the crown be discharged.

The nearest that the rebels came to an attack on the King himself concerned the supremacy in the Church, of which they asked that cure of souls 'be restored unto the See of Rome as before it was accustomed to be'. It is likely that this article too was submitted on the initiative of Robert Aske. All other criticisms were made not in the direction of the King but towards Thomas Cromwell, a useful whipping-boy whose influence and importance enabled the rebels to equate their opposition to recent changes with loyalty to their King. Criticism of Cromwell therefore permeates the Pontefract articles deeply. Even the demand that Mary be made legitimate and that the statute of the declaration of the crown by will be repealed can be seen to derive from a naive fear that Cromwell might be made heir to the throne. On a more realistic footing, the rebels demanded that Cromwell and his clients 'have condign punishment as the subverters of the good laws of this realm. . .'. Similarly Cromwell's monastic visitors, Layton and Legh, were criticised for the 'abominable acts by them committed and done'. Despite the omission of the article submitted at York which attacked 'persons as be of low birth and small reputation which hath procured the profits most especially for their own advantage', the implication that counsel should stem from men of noble birth remains. Other grievances of the gentlemen leaders of the rebellion were spelled out with more emphasis. These concerned the statute of uses, the statute of treason by words, the reformation of elections to parliament and parliamentary procedure, the discharge of the subsidy (which article, although receiving popular support, concerned only those with an annual income of over £20), and recent changes in common law practice.

The disadvantage of living in the north of England was another theme developed by the Pontefract articles. This grievance may to some extent be seen in the demand that the liberties of the church be restored in northern towns such as Durham, Ripon and York, and later in the Doncaster articles in the request to have more northern burgesses in Parliament. More significantly, the disparity between north and south is applied to the law in a demand that any man living north of the Trent should be able to answer a subpoena at York rather than London unless the case at issue concerned treason. Most of all, the grievances of northerners appear in the demand for a parliament at Nottingham or York, a demand which eventually the King was able to latch upon and exploit to the full.

If these grievances derived primarily from gentlemen, those of the commons also appeared in the Pontefract articles. The complaints of the north-west concerning tenant-right and payment of entry fines, enclosures and the payment of feudal dues such as neat-geld were included.

These, the most important of the Pontefract articles, show the diversity of rebel demands. What they do not show is the whole range of rebel grievance, a subject which still requires study in its own right. The York articles, the Pontefract articles, and the Doncaster articles (which latter added to the Pontefract demands the call for a pardon for all who had taken part in the Pilgrimage of Grace) demonstrate in no order of priority those grievances which the rebels chose to commit to paper. If the rebellion in the north-east and Yorkshire was also an attempt by the Percy family and their clients to bolster their dwindling influence at the expense of the King or rival factions, the conspirators are hardly likely to have said so.[2] If the rebellion was a belated attempt by the Earl of Northumberland, Lord Darcy and others to stir a Catholic rising against the King which would be supported by Spain, such a plan was covert, and considering the tenor of the rest of the rebellion, stillborn. If the rebellion was a class war, then at least in the first instance the classes found that they had enough in common to bring them mutual advantage by alliance.

The rebel articles tell us nothing about these broader implications of the rebellion. Neither do they tell us of minor issues such as personal vendettas which no doubt were carried out in the name of rebellion.

The title 'Pilgrimage of Grace', the badge of five wounds, and other trappings of a religious crusade demonstrate the grievances of

[2]Some of the broader implications of the rebellion are dealt with in the introduction, above pp. 1-4.

the rebellion at their most emotive level. Beneath that, the rebellion meant a multiplicity of things to each individual, faction, or region which took part. The answer to the problem of rebel grievance is a complex one even for the one region of the Lake Counties.

Economic Grievances

A study of the economy of the Lake Counties in the sixteenth century has shown that the region was one of great poverty. This poverty was exacerbated by more wide-ranging events. Before 1530 there was a considerable price inflation, and the pressure which this put on landlords was certainly transmitted to the tenants. In years of plenty such pressures could be borne, but harvest failure was certain to reveal the dissatisfaction of the tenantry. The years 1535-6 and 1536-7 were ones of poor harvest and high prices in the Lake Counties. However, such things should be regarded as precipitants rather than grievances. The rebels were unable to fight dearth itself, but what they could do was turn their attention towards the tangible manifestations of encroachment on their livelihood. Some of their economic complaints were directed against the permanent charges on their wealth, such as tithes. Others were against those recent enhancements which may have been introduced by lords to keep in step with rising prices. These included the raising of entry fines, the enclosing of land for improvement, and the exploitation of the traditional tenure of cornage.

Entry Fines

By far the greatest volume of the rebels' economic complaint was directed against the raising of entry fines or gressums, the payments made by most copyholders at a change of lord or tenant. At Kendal the rebels demanded that all tenants should 'take your farms by a God's Penny, all gressums and heightnings [raises of fines] to be laid down'; at Kirkby Stephen the commons desired that 'the gressums for poor men to be laid apart, but only penny farm penny gressum'; and in Cumberland, the Duke of Norfolk referred to 'the gressing of them so marvellously sore in time past' as a principal cause of the insurrection there.[3] Gressums, therefore, were deeply resented not only in the strongest rebel areas, but throughout the Lake Counties. On this issue, at least, the commons were completely united.

Three types of entry fines or gressum can be identified. Strictly speaking an entry fine was paid by a tenant on his accession to an estate. A copyholder paid an entry fine once, a leaseholder at the

[3]*LP*,XI, 892 (3); PRO, S.P.I, III, p. 134 (*LP*,XI, 1030); *LP*,XII(1), 478.

termination of each of his lives. A gressum was paid at the change of lord, either through sale or death. Usually, entry fines and gressums were the same in quantity, and the distinction of terminology was rarely made. Thirdly, some communities had to pay a running gressum. Often this was paid in lieu of other fines, but otherwise it was paid by a township for a piece of land held in common, as was the case at Dent. A running gressum was paid by the tenants at fixed intervals. Entry fines and gressums were unpredictable and might occur with frequency or at long intervals. However, the threat of a gressum was ever-present to the tenant, and that of an entry fine to the heir to a tenement. The extent of the fine was thus a constant concern to the inhabitants of the Lake Counties, and an enhancement of the fine provided an immediate threat to all tenants, however distant their next payment might seem to be. Irregularity of payment in terms of time was not the only variable. Throughout the region customs differed considerably, some providing security to the tenant, others the opportunity for profit to the lord. Amongst the former were Borrowdale and Holm Cultram. At Borrowdale the entry fine due was one year's rent. At change of lord only a God's Penny (signifying that a bargain had been struck) was paid.[4] The same situation existed at Holm Cultram but for the existence of a five-yearly running gressum, and at Dent where a God's Penny and a Clerk's Penny were payable, plus a running gressum known as 'town tearmes'.[5] In 1634 this was worth the considerable sum of £72 6s. 0d., divided amongst the tenants, payable in three years after every change of lord, and in 'every eighth year after the cessation of seven years'. Possibly this fine had been enhanced, but at least the period of payment was fixed.

An entry fine of one year's rent, and a gressum of a God's Penny were demanded from the most fortunate tenants. During the sixteenth century there was considerable enhancement of fines, but it is evident that as early as 1536 an entry fine and gressum of two years' rent was commonplace. At Ennerdale and certain of the Kendal manors a fixed fine of two years rent was stipulated, as well as at Bampton and two other manors of the Barony of Westmorland.[6] Two years' rent was also paid for fines on most of the Percy manors, although the bulk were arbitrable and thus likely to be subjected to early enhancements.[7]

[4]PRO, D.L. 44, no. 333.

[5]Joint Archive, Carlisle, Book of Papers relating to Holm Cultram, 41; and Joint Archive, Kendal, copy of Court of Exchequer proceedings, 1634-41, relating to Dent; and Joint Archive, Kendal, ibid.

[6]R.P. Littledale, 'Ennerdale', CWAAS, new ser., 31, pp. 156-96; J. Nicholson and R. Burn, The History and Antiquities of the Counties of Westmorland and Cumberland (London, 1777), Vol. I, pp. 335-46, 350.

[7]Bean, pp. 51-8.

Manors where arbitrary fines were applicable included Castlerigg, Seaton, Thornthwaite, and Bassenthwaite in Cumberland, and Kirkby Stephen, Brough, and the bulk of the Barony of Westmorland. Elsewhere fines were already high; witness a court case in dispute of right to a tenement in Furness. In 1533 Leonard Braithwaite and others were accused of driving away three hundred sheep and destroying the hedges around a tenement of 460 acres at Graythwaite.[8] In his own defence Braithwaite stated that he had been given a moiety of this land by the late William Dixon, who had paid for the whole £1 6s. 4d. and a gressum at the change of tenant. The gressum that Braithwaite had to pay to enter the tenement was £6 13s. 4d., which on a moiety of the original property was an entry fine of ten years rent. Although no gressum was payable, this represented an extremely high payment which other landlords attempted to equal in succeeding years.

Entry fines and gressums were most likely to rise where payments were not fixed. However, even stipulated fines were threatened where the tenant's right to enter a property was in doubt. In fact this was rarely the case in the Lake Counties. Where a tenant held land by custom (leaseholders were few in the region) it was generally accepted that the tenure included tenant right, even if this was not written into an agreement. This tenant right was 'tantamount to freehold', entitling individuals to bequeath land as they desired, take mortgages, and within certain limits use the land as they wished.[9] Even men who were strictly tenants at will, 'in the main, we take it, were really customary tenants'. However, being able to prove one's right was another matter, and where tenant right was uncertain, a tenant challenged by his lord may well have consented to a higher gressum rather than risk an expensive court case or eviction through lack of written title.

During the rebellion the commons did not demand an abolition of gressums and entry fines, which were a normal and accepted part of their tenancies. In the official rebel demand made at Doncaster, which no doubt represented a compromise between the lowly representatives of the Lake Counties and the lords responsible for enhancements, a clear statement of intent was made:

> Item that the landes in Westmorland, Cumberland, Kendall, Dent, Sedber, Fornes, and abbeys landes in Mashamshire Kyrkbyshire, Notherdale may be by tenant right, and the lord to have at every change ii years rent for gressum and no more

[8] PRO, D.L.3/25/F.1.
[9] Bouch and Jones, p. 69.

according to the grant now made by the lords to the commons there under their seal. And this to be done by act of parliament.[10]

The rebels of the Lake Counties were less compromising in their original demands, considering a fine of one year's rent or a God's Penny to be sufficient. There can be little doubt that this was a reaction to recent enhancements which were occurring throughout the region, both in the quantity of money demanded and the frequency of exaction.[11]

A coincidence of land transfers was the basic cause of dissatisfaction on the Percy estates. Evidence for these estates is incomplete, and statistics for some years are entirely lacking. However, receipts in a 'normal' year such as 1521-2 totalled £38 18s. 8d., or £37 12s. 6¼d. in 1523-4.[12] These figures represent the payments of entry fines at change of tenant. In 1527 the sixth Earl of Northumberland entered into his estates, and a gressum from all tenants became due. In 1530 the Cumberland manors of Dean, Whinfell, Great and Little Broughton, Caldbeck Underfell, and Birkby were granted in tail male to Sir Thomas Wharton, who was entitled to receive a further gressum. In 1531 the honour of Cockermouth was granted to the King, and in that year gressums of £311 7s. 5d. were recorded, the second sum of this magnitude to have become due in four years. Pressure on the tenants did not cease with the transfer of the estates to the King, for in 1535 they were returned to the Earl to assist with the security of the northern borders. Not only did a further gressum become due, but yet another was threatened, for the Earl declared in February 1536 that the King was to be his heir, and the Earl's state of health made the transfer imminent.[13] In fact, he died a little over a year later, in June 1537. It is not certain whether all the gressums that were due were in fact collected. If they were, then all ex-Percy lands in Cumberland were subjected to two gressums in four years, and those in the Barony of Cockermouth to four gressums in ten years, these being in addition to any entry fines that the tenants may have paid during the period. Even on the assumption that an average of one entry fine was paid during the ten years, the total of extra payments effectively doubled the rent.

Fortunately the extent of the gressum on the Percy estates was moderate, despite the fact that fines were arbitrary. Fines at this time

---

[10]*LP*, XI, 1246.

[11]*Ibid.*, XI, 1080.

[12]Bean, p. 66.

[13]*LP*, X, 150.

were levied at a rate of between one and one and a half year's rent. This was a higher figure than had been charged in the fifteenth century, but the enhancements seem to have occurred in the early fifteen-twenties and were quite acceptable in comparison with fines elsewhere. Neither does there appear to have been a policy of outright exploitation of their tenants by the fifth or sixth Earls. The vague tenant right which existed on Percy estates was not undermined, and there was no attempt to instigate the practice of substituting leases for copyhold. In fact, it would be surprising if this had been the case in the light of the sixth Earl's ineptitude in managing his estates.

The animosity towards gressums on the Cumberland estates was therefore largely a product of the coincidence of exactions of gressums during the decade preceding the rebellion, due to 'personal and political factors' which concerned the sixth Earl. No doubt it was this to which Norfolk referred when he noted 'the gressing of them so marvellously sore in time past'.[14] In 1537 Robert Southwell examined the books of account for gressums and assessed the value to the King as one thousand marks from the Percy estates. However, he was loathe to collect them as it would 'gratify the tenants more than it would have done before' if the payment were remitted.[15] The lands granted to Sir Thomas Wharton posed a different problem. Southwell assessed the value of the gressums there as another five hundred marks, but deferred judgement on them to the King, as Wharton had enhanced them considerably already. Since the transfer of 1530 Wharton must have raised the entry fines on the estates, which would explain the great animosity of tenants towards him during the rebellion.

Wharton's enhancing of fines was more the rule than the exception. This is demonstrated by the change in estate policy made by William Lord Dacre in 1535. An extremely feudal relationship existed between the Lords Dacre and their tenants before that time. This was essential on lands so close to the border, where loyalty to one's lord was necessary for communal defence and self-preservation. Dacre appears to have maintained the unstinting support of his tenantry, and no direct economic complaint issued from his estates during the rebellion.[16] However, even Lord Dacre had enhanced his gressums in 1535, a fact which may have driven his tenants closer to the other rebels. In that year Sir Christopher Dacre and the officers on all the estates in Cumberland and Westmorland were instructed to

---

[14]*Ibid.*, XII(1), 478.

[15]*Ibid.*, XII(2), 548.

[16]For the relationship between Lord Dacre and his tenants see pp. 39-40

make certain improvements in their management, including the raising of decayed rents, the confirmation of tenants' titles, the re establishment of subdivided tenements, and the elimination of corruption amongst officers.[17] The most important changes concerned gressums. Lord Dacre commanded that they 'do let all my said lands after the rate of three years rent for the fine and gressum of their tenements and to be paid in three years following'. Exceptions were made, officers not having to demand 'fine or gressum of all such persons that hath contented and agreed with me since I entered unto my lands except they may be lovingly induced there unto'. Furthermore, if a tenement became vacant, Dacre ordered 'that my commissioners do let the same to a person being a good archer and able for the serving of the King's highness and rather to him for lesser gressum than to any other being no archer'. However, even such examples of benevolence can hardly have lessened the impact of increased gressums for the bulk of the Dacre tenantry.

The examples of Dacre and Wharton seem to have been adopted (if not inspired) by the gentlemen of Cumberland. One case that reached the courts at London concerned the notorious Peter Middleton of Castlerigg.[18] In 1531 the manor of Castlerigg was demised to Middleton by Richard Debenside, the second husband of Alice Ratcliffe. The lands had descended to Dame Alice from Sir John Ratcliffe, and the right of Debenside to grant the manor away was in contention. Middleton maintained his hold on the estates and demanded of his tenants a gressum which they owed for the change of lord at the time of Sir John Ratcliffe's death. The stated custom of the manor was that 'at any time of transmission of possession either of the lord or of the tenant that the tenant or tenants shall pay such reasonable fine or gressom as the lord and he can agree'.[19] In other words, fines were arbitrary, and the gressum demanded from each tenant was four marks. In the sense that no base figure is recorded, the gressum charged may have been one of four years' rent. Certainly the incident prompted Dame Alice to add to her charges against Middleton the fact that he was bothering the tenants.[20] As well as charging full entry fines, Middleton was evicting tenants at will, whether they had paid their entry fines or not. One leaseholder, Alan Bunting, was kept out of his rightful property by Middleton, who was supporting the entry of Christopher Wilkinson.[21] During the

[17]Durham, Department of Palaeography and Diplomatic. C/201/5.

[18]PRO. C.1. 853/43.

[19] *Ibid.*

[20]PRO. C.1. 878/6-7.

[21]*Ibid.*, C.1. 727/12.

Pilgrimage of Grace Middleton, like Wharton, was to suffer at the hands of his tenants for the harsh estate policies which he had pursued during the preceding years.[22]

Westmorland estates were also subjected to increasing entry fines and gressums. At Kendal the only evidence of increasing gressums can be found in the rebel complaints. When news of the rebellion came to Kendal the first act of the rebels was to go to the house of Sir James Layburn. They asked him 'to be good to them concerning their laudable customs', saying that there was no reason that where his father took four marks for a gressum he should take forty pounds.[23] The implication that Layburn had been levying entry fines of fifteen years' rent is almost beyond belief. More probably the rebels were speaking figuratively. Possibly they even confused their units, for a fine of ten years' rent was not considered unreasonable in later years. Whatever the answer, the rebels asked that Layburn should practise on his lands as Sir William Parr and the King did on their nearby estates, for otherwise less sympathetic lords such as the Bellinghams and Stricklands might follow his example. Kendal was particularly susceptible to rises in entry fine, both because of uncertainty of tenure and of the extent of the payments. A survey of 1572 stated that 'the tenants have neither copy nor other evidence to show for their titles'.[24] Although a fine of double the rent was stipulated, this could have been raised by an attack on the custom of the manor. Moreover, a case in chancery of 1607 demonstrates how fines were increased.[25] This case questioned not only the custom by which tenants entered their estates, but also whether the entry fines and gressums were fixed or arbitrary. The practice of charging a gressum on the death of the lord was described by the commission as 'very beneficial to their lords'. Evidently conflict had by this time grown to great proportions, and in order 'to settle an universal peace between the said lords and tenants being very many and poor . . . we recommend the settling of the fines at some certain rate'. Thus certainty was not established in the Barony of Kendal until 1607. At the time of the Pilgrimage of Grace the rebels' demand that they should 'claim the old customs and tenant right to take your farms by God's penny, all gressums and heightnings to be laid down' reflected the knowledge that insecurity was providing Layburn and possibly other lords with the opportunity to raise their fines.[26]

[22] See below, pp. 110-1

[23] *LP*, XII(1), 914.

[24] Nicholson and Burn, 1, 45-6.

[25] Joint Archives, Kendal, Mason-Hornby Papers, copy of this case.

[26] *LP*, XI, 892(3).

The Barony of Westmorland was prominent in the struggle against gressums. Only at Drybeck, Little Asby and Bampton were fines fixed. Of the mesne tenants it has already been shown that Lord Dacre and Sir Thomas Wharton were raising their fines. Most important, however, was the policy of the Earl of Cumberland.

In a survey of Clifford's knight's fees dated 1526 a note was added which introduced new entry fines.[27] In the forests of Stainmore and Mallerstang new tenants were to be charged with an entry fine of seven or eight years' rent. In townships new tenants were to pay an entry fine of five years' rent. Older tenants were to be rated at four years' rent in the forests and three years' rent in the towns. Even the lowest of these enhancements was relatively severe by comparison with other estates. A complete set of bailiffs' rolls does not exist, but even so it is possible to prove that the new policy was initiated before the Pilgrimage of Grace. Fortunately bailiffs' rolls do exist for the years 1534 and 1541-2, and entered therein is the income from gressums (by which is meant entry fines) on the Clifford estates in Westmorland. They are compared in Table 3.[28]

These statistics have certain limitations. The total number of fines is small, and some large payments upset the average payment for the parish, as in the case of Mallerstang and Sowerby. However, in both of these cases the total is comprised of several half payments in 1534. If these payments were doubled, the total for Sowerby would be £12 1s. 0d., and for Mallerstang £5 15s. 11½d. In both cases the total for the parish would then be comparable with 1542. Despite these failings, the remarkable similarity of average payments for entry fines indicates that policy was the same in 1534 as in 1542, and therefore the Earl of Cumberland's enhancements must already have taken place before the Pilgrimage of Grace.

Significance must also be attached to the number of men hanged for their part in the rebellion who paid gressums to the Earl of Cumberland in 1534.[29] Hugh Dent paid a fine of £1 3s. 3½d., and William Shaw paid the first part of a payment worth twelve shillings. Both were hanged at Mallerstang in 1537.[30] Peter Johnson of Kirkby Stephen paid half of his fine of £2 10s. 4d., the rest of which was due in

[27] James, 'First Earl of Cumberland', p. 53, note 56. I have been unable to locate this document, which is partly transcribed by James in this article.

[28] The 1534 roll is amongst the manuscripts of his Grace the Duke of Devonshire, the Library, Chatsworth, Vol. 10. The 1542 roll of which the head is missing, is in the Joint Archives, Kendal.

[29] Chatsworth, Volume 10.

[30] See below, pp. 125-6.

Table 3: Income from entry fines on Clifford estates

Parish	1534			1542		
	No. of fines	Total Income (£ s. d.)	Average Income (£ s. d.)	No. of fines	Total Income (£ s. d.)	Average Income (£ s. d.)
Mallerstang	4	3 9 7½	17 5	2	5 11. 0	2 15 6
Brough	2	1 7 4	13 8	8	5 1 10	12 6
Sowerby	6	9 12 2	1 12 0	5	12 4 0	2 8 10
Stainmore	7	4 0 10	11 7	13	9 14 7	15 0
Appleby	4	4 2 8	1 0 8	1	1 2 4	1 2 4
Kirkby Stephen	3	7 10 4	2 10 1	1	1 18 5½	1 18 5½
King's Meaburn	1	1 2 2½	1 2 2½	0	00 0	00 0
Totals	27	31 5 2	1 3 2	30	35 12 2½	1 3 8

1535. He too was hanged at Mallerstang. John Hall paid the whole of his fine of £2 13s. 4d. He was hanged at Appleby. Both Robert and Henry Wilkyn of Sowerby paid fines, totalling thirteen shillings and fourpence and six shillings and eight pence respectively. Another Wilkyn, William of Sowerby, was hanged there in 1537. From a total of twenty-seven men who had paid fines in 1534-5, four were directly connected with rebellion, and one other had namesakes paying gressums. Three of them came from the manor of Mallerstang which suffered most from Clifford enhancements, and one of them, Peter Johnson, was also linked with the rebellious community of Kirkby Stephen. He may have had to contribute to the running gressum of £1 18s. 5½d. for a piece of land held in common. This sum was paid in 1542, and if, as in nearby Dent, the gressum was paid on a seven-year basis, it would have also been due in 1535. All of these men were prominent in the rebel ranks; otherwise the Duke of Norfolk would not have singled them out for retribution.[31] There can be little doubt that their participation was strongly tied to resentment against paying these fines.

Whether by frequency of exaction or by recent enhancement the peasants of the Lake Counties were hard pressed by entry fines and gressums in the decade leading up to the Pilgrimage of Grace. In 1569 it was remarked after the failure of the northern Earls' rising that the commons, 'their duties and fines being certain . . . will not be led . . . to rebellion'.[32] Of the economic grievances of 1536, entry fines were by far the most important, and the complaint of the rebels can be seen as the first shots in a battle which was to last for many years.

Tithes

A further economic grievance concerned the payment of tithes. People in the sixteenth century seem to have complained about tithes in the same way that their descendants complain about income tax today. Tithes were a long-standing grievance, and one which was the subject of vast quantities of litigation in the local and central courts.[33] Accepting this, it may seem contentious to include complaints against tithes as motives for rebellion. In normal circumstances, criticism of tithes could only be seen as a routine affair, somewhat exacerbated by years of dearth. Apart from the natural shortage of corn in the Lake Counties, there is no reason to believe that tithes were a greater problem there than elsewhere. The complaint which

[31]*LP*, XII(1), 498.

[32]Bouch and Jones, p. 73.

[33]C. Hill, *Economic Problems of the Church*, Part II, Chapter Five.

was made concerning tithes can best be explained by the fact that the rebels were criticizing particular aspects of tithe farming and that they seem to have wanted to find a reasonable solution to the problem.

There can be no doubt that the rebels were willing to pay tithes. The most extreme demand made during the Pilgrimage of Grace was that the rebels 'wanted to pay no rent nor tithe but in money at their pleasure'.[34] However, in their own manifesto the rebels of Westmorland asked that 'all tythes to remain to every man his own, doing therefore according to their duty'.[35] In other words, the peasants accepted the obligation of tithes. What they resented were two aspects of the mechanism of tithe collection which were particularly obnoxious to them. The first concerned the practice of tithe-farming by laymen, and the second the hardship which was caused by the removal of the great tithe, the tenth of corn, in an area where corn was always scarce.

The practice of tithe farming was performed on behalf of absentee priests and of distant monasteries to which a tithe had been appropriated. There can be no doubt that the farming of tithes was an extremely profitable affair, and disputes between the farmers appear to have been frequent.

In 1528 the Abbot of Furness brought a case against William Redmayne before the court of Star Chamber.[36] Redmayne had farmed the tithe of Urswick for twenty years until, in 1527, his lease expired. In both that year and in 1528 Redmayne took the tithe of Urswick, saying that the lease still continued. In 1535 a dispute between tithe farmers occurred at Langrigg.[37] The Abbey of St. Mary's at York had leased the tithe of Langrigg to three husbandmen, Anthony Eaglesfield, Edward Roper and John Thornbrand. A part of the lease had then been sold to William Osmonderley, who farmed his share of the tithe for seven years until 1535, at which time Roper and Thornbrand not only took away tithe corn, but also corn from Osmonderley's own estate. In the replication to this case, Osmonderley was accused of not paying for his share of the tithe, but taking more of the corn than was his by right. Thornbrand and Roper also held a lease of tithes in Bromfield and Allonby, again from St. Mary's York. In an undated court of Chancery case they accused one John Martindale of breaking an agreement which they had made concerning a portion of the tithe.[38] This portion amounted to £3 in value, and Martindale

[34]PRO. S.P.1., 117. pp. 46-69. (*LP*, XII(1). 687(1).)

[35]*LP*. XI. 1080.

[36]PRO. STAC.2. 19/129-31.

[37]*Ibid.*, 27/105.

[38]*Ibid.*, 916/28.

only appears to have had to pay twenty shillings in return, which he had failed to do. If one assumes that these were great tithes of corn, Martindale was realising a considerable profit for service in which he had merely to cut, transport, store and sell the crop.

Considering the original purpose of tithes, these cases and others of the time show that the practice of appropriating tithes led to rather sordid profiteering. The tithe was a regressive tax hitting hardest at the people who farmed arable land only at subsistence level. Occasionally direct action was taken against tithes and tithe farmers to alleviate the problem. In 1534 and 1535 a number of persons stole the tithe corn of Skelton, worth £2 3s. 4d., from Thomas Talentire.[39] In 1536 the parishoners of St. Theobald's at Carlisle refused to pay their tithes, saying that they had already been taken by Sir William Musgrave.[40] The Chancellor to the Bishop of Carlisle, Barnard Towneley, gave little credence to this story and recommended that action be taken against them. An undated case, but one which took place during the chancellorship of Thomas Audley (1532-44), shows that at Brigham the parishioners also refused payment of tithes. However, on this occasion the refusal was absolute, and the accused parties said that in future they would pay tithe-corn only at their own pleasure.[41]

The evidence of complaint against tithes which was expressed during the Pilgrimage of Grace specifies the objects of discontent. The first of these was the tithe farmers. It has been suggested that the great tithes were a particular source of resentment because they had lost their spiritual function. The tithe had been leased to men who may have also collected seignorial rents, either as landlord or farmer of the monastic demesne. It is significant that the tithe barns that were raided in Cumberland during the course of the rebellion were owned by two of the most notorious landlords, Sir Thomas Wharton and Peter Middleton. In January 1537, 'the tenants of Broughton did put out the threshers of Sir Thos. Wharton out of "teyth laythe" at Broughton and did set one lock on the door'.[42] Thomas Lamplugh attempted to negotiate with four of the rebels' leaders, but 'all your other tenants did go to the barn . . . and your corn and hay divided and dealt your corn among them'.[43] Middleton's barn was attacked on the following day, and similar action was threatened at Broughton, Seaton, and Eaglesfield. Attacks continued into February, at which time the Duke of Norfolk wrote of Cockermouth that 'there rose there

[39]*Ibid.*, 30/112.

[40]*LP*, X, 96.

[41]PRO, C.1., 924/70.

[42]*LP*, XII(1), 18.

[43]PRO, S.P.1., 114, p. 20 (*LP*, XII(1), 18).

about eight hundred and made their quarrel to take everyman his corn that he had tithed, and would have the same for their money, and so took all that was in the tithe barns in the country without paying anything therefore'.[44]

In these cases the spiritual aspect of tithes does not seem to have been considered by either side. The corn was held by two gentlemen who had mistreated their tenants and had raised entry fines whenever possible.[45] Not only did the rioters on these occasions have the gratification of reclaiming much needed corn, but they were also striking a blow against their landlords who had disappeared from the region.

The men of Westmorland, who seem to have been more concerned with religious aspects of the rebellion than their neighbours in Cumberland, were rather more discriminating in their assault on tithes. In the case of the parish of Heversham in Kendal, the commons 'withheld their tithes from the farmers who had leased them from the Abbot of St. Mary's'.[46] Here, the tithe farmers appear to have been regarded as middle-men, and the root of the problem lay in the possession of benefices by distant abbeys which offered little or nothing in return. St. Mary's, York in particular derived large incomes from the Lake Counties. Tithes of the vicarages of Kirkby Lonsdale, Kendal, Burton, Bromfield, Morland, Kirkby Stephen and the rectories of Windermere, Grasmere and Brigham all went to St. Mary's. Other institutions holding benefices in the Lake Counties included the Abbeys of Coverham, Rosedale, Gisburn, Fountains, and Croxton.[47] Often the value of benefices was small, but the spiritual income of Kendal amounted to £84 18s. 4d., and that of Kirkby Stephen to £46 15s. 2d. St. Mary's alone collected £17 9s. 4d. in temporal income, and £202 6s. 0d. in spiritual income from the Lake Counties.

The rebels also complained about the abuses of absenteeism. The commons were keen to take absentee clerics, such as Parson Threlkeld of Melmerby who held three benefices. They also 'determined to take the fruits of the benefices of all them that were absent'.[48] Amongst these the rebels may have included those who

---

[44]*LP*, XII(1), 319.

[45]See below, pp. 110-1.

[46]*LP*, XII(1),671(3).

[47]*Valor*, V, pp. 259-60, 265-8, 272, 283-92, 294-8. For example, Covernham held Sedbergh, Rosedale held Torpenhow, Gisburn held Dearham, Fountains held Crosthwaite, and Croxton held Tunstall.

[48]*LP*, XII(1), 687(2).

were 'no priests that hath the benefice in hand' and 'my Lord Cromwell chaplains'. In their place they wanted men who would serve God, and by implication, earn the tithes that were due to them.

Rebel resentment against the receivers of tithes who were unworthy of their office, and concern that the tithe of corn was an immense burden on an area where corn was scarce, motivated the Pilgrims in the Lake Counties to look for a practical solution to the problem. The complaint against tithes included in the manifesto from the Barony of Westmorland went unanswered, so in January 1537 an invitation to go to Richmond, supposedly to discuss the problem of tithes with the Duke of Norfolk, was greeted with enthusiasm.[49] The several representatives who were sent into Yorkshire found that the meeting was a fabrication. Neither Norfolk nor any gentleman of significance was there. However, the rebels must be credited with the attempt to find a useful settlement.

In Ket's rebellion of 1549 tithes were named as a grievance by the rebels, but they seem to have been added to an already long list just for the sake of it.[50] In the Lake Counties tithes must be seen as a sincere complaint which came from several parts of the region. However, it would be wrong to say that the rebels were concerned with tithes 'above all', and to generalise to the effect that 'a rebellion which plundered all the tithe barns on which it could lay hands . . . could scarcely be inflated into a crusade for the rights of Holy Church'.[51] The pilgrims in the Lake Counties complained about tithes on social and economic grounds; they were not in any sense attacking the church. At their most radical they were taking tithe corn in time of shortage from the barns where it had been stored by unpopular landlords. More moderate rebels, especially those of Westmorland, were trying to negotiate a mutually acceptable solution to modify and improve rather than abolish a system which had already been corrupted by wealthy laymen and clerics alike.

Enclosure

Amongst the rebel articles submitted at Doncaster for the King's consideration was a request for 'the Statute for inclosures and intacks to be put in execution, and all enclosures and intacks since Henry VII to be pulled down except mountains, forests and parks'.[52] In the Lake District the official complaint against enclosures was specifically

[49]*Ibid.*, 671(3).

[50]See S.T. Bindoff, *Ket's Rebellion, 1549,* Historical Association (1949).

[51]Dickens, 'Secular and Religious Motivation', p. 51.

[52]*LP,* XI, 1246.

supported by one statement. In their letter to Lord Darcy, Nicholas Musgrave and Robert Pulleyn expressed a wish to have 'all the intakes that are noysum for poor men to be laid down'.[53]

In the absence of any greater volume of complaint concerning enclosures in the Lake Counties, it is necessary to ask how far they were a real issue, and what form any physical demonstrations against enclosures took. It has been written of the Lake Counties 'that there was little interest in our region during the sixteenth century on account of the enclosure of open fields, and . . . there was less disturbance than occurred elsewhere because of enclosing of commons, of which there was a much greater extent available'.[54] Generally speaking an area already dominated by wool and with grain in short supply saw little conversion from arable to pasture. Often communities saw no need to stint their infield grazing, and intakes were permitted.[55] A survey at Castle Sowerby conducted in 1585 established that 'the steward and his deputy could grant and let by copy of court roll according to the custom such wastes, moors and common pastures to be improved as were not to the annoyance or hurt of the other tenants'.[56] An indifferent jury of villagers was appointed to decide on the desirability of each case of proposed improvement. At Sadgill in Kendal no stint had been laid down by 1582, a deposition of which date stated that 'time out of mind the commons had been open to all without interuption'.[57] These two instances are typical of the situation throughout the Lake Counties. Only the narrow valley communities, the more densely populated and more fertile regions such as Furness, the Eden Valley and parts of the Cumberland coast, had an enclosure problem.

The courts of Star Chamber, Chancery and the Duchy of Lancaster dealt with enclosure cases of three types that related to the Lake Counties: enclosure for purposes of conversion to pasture; encroachment on the common wastes; and the denial of traditional infield grazing rights.

The only evidence of enclosure for the purposes of conversion to pasture relates to Furness Abbey. The abbots of Furness appear to have pursued a consistent policy of this nature, presumably to cash in on the healthy profits associated with the wool trade. In 1516 William and Isabel Caase accused Abbot Banke of Furness of evicting the

[53]*Ibid.*. 1080.

[54]Bouch and Jones. pp. 76-7.

[55]See above. p. 13.

[56]PRO. E.134, 26 Eliz. Mich.9.

[57]*Ibid.*. 23 Eliz. Hil.9.

customary tenants of Roose and Selergarth.[58]   On 16 December Banke and twenty-two monks turned out the occupants of a total of fifty-two tenements. Subsequently all these were pulled down, and a third of the arable land which had been attached to the tenements was enclosed and converted to pasture, causing the decay of thirteen ploughs. Other tenants at Sandetalle, Southend and Wanaxe had suffered the same fate. Abbot Pyle continued with the policies of Banke. When he refused the gressum of Leonard Braithwaite, a customary tenant by tenant right, and attempted to graze three hundred of his sheep on the land there Braithwaite threw down his enclosures.[59]   No evidence exists to show that the tenants of the abbey expressed their hatred of enclosures during the Pilgrimage of Grace. Perhaps loyalty to the abbey came first, or the close proximity of the abbey inhibited the tenants. Only in 1535 can one find evidence of dissatisfaction, and that on the more distant Yorkshire estates in Craven. On that occasion fourteen tenants of the abbey were arrested for their part in a large-scale riot mainly involving the tenants of the Earl of Cumberland.[60]

Their intention was to pull down enclosures which encroached on the commons, and possibly this was motivated by the fact that they had received the same treatment from the abbey as had their counterparts in Furness.

Cumberland does not appear to have been the scene for many enclosure disputes. Riots were confined to attacks on the estates of two local gentlemen. John Legh, a Dacre client who held land at Frizington, which was thus an enclave in Percy territory, appears to have been making consistent encroachments on the common land. In 1534 rioters threw down the hedge around his close at Crewgarth,[61] and in 1535 the inhabitants of Cleator and Frizington rose against his intakes on the moorland.[62]   Possibly these riots were stimulated as much by malice as by economic hardship. Legh was a hard landlord, and when he tried to obtain the sheriffwick of Cumberland in 1531[63] he assured the King that his first priority would be to enforce the King's rights against local freeholders by cornage.[64]   As well as being unpopular with tenants and freeholders, he was opposed by local

[58]PRO, D.L.1., Vol. II, C.3.

[59]PRO, D.L.3., 25, F.1.

[60]LP, VIII, 863.

[61]PRO, STAC.2, 1/44-5.

[62]LP, VIII, 1133.

[63]Ibid., V, 1447.

[64]See below, pp. 69-70.

gentlemen, and in the aftermath of the Pilgrimage of Grace Sir Thomas Curwen and others attempted to implicate him in the rising.[65] John Legh's connection with his cousin Dr Thomas Legh, the notorious visitor of the monasteries, may have increased his unpopularity, and the throwing down of enclosures in this case may have been no more than a personal attack.

Robert Briscow, a regular contender at the central courts, also had his enclosures attacked. An undated Star Chamber case relates to a dispute at Dundraw.[66] Briscow complained that Adam Watson, William Langrigg and about sixty-five other persons had entered his close and cast down his hedges. In a comprehensive reply Langrigg complained that Sir Roger Cholmeley, the tenant in chief of the manor, had always reserved the common land for the use of the tenants at will. Therefore such tenants were within their rights to pull down the hedges and graze stock on the common land. A counter-accusation complained that Briscow had assembled forty men on horseback who had ridden to the land in question and stolen six oxen, six cows, a steer and a mare. Some of these had since been destroyed, and no compensation had been given. The case at Dundraw was clearly a matter of dispute between the conflicting interests of Briscow and the tenants at will. However, like John Legh, Robert Briscow was subject to riots of a political nature. In 1532 he was expelled from his property,[67] and in an undated case, probably relating to 1535, over two hundred people attacked his property and stole his grass.[68] His attackers were Dacre servants, and Briscow himself was a deputy to the Earl of Cumberland. The connection between this fact and enclosures is that the Cliffords and their allies appear to have pursued a consistent policy of enclosure, and these improvements became targets for rioters whose motives were both economic and political.

The Cliffords dominated the Barony of Westmorland, part of which consisted of the Eden Valley. This area was more fertile and more populous than most parts of the Lake Counties, and consequently pressure on land was greater. Evidence has survived of two separate types of dispute which occurred there prior to the Pilgrimage of Grace. At Temple Sowerby the issue in contention was the right to grazing on the infield.[69] Sometime before 1524 John and James

[65] *LP,* XII(1), 904.

[66] PRO, STAC.2, 6/370.

[67] *Ibid.,* 6/96-7.

[68] *Ibid.,* 6/263.

[69] *Ibid.,* 31/44.

Crackenthorpe were accused of wrongs and oppressions committed against the tenants of the hospital of St. John. Whereas the tenants had always been allowed to graze their cattle on the common cornfields after harvest had been gathered, this privilege had now been removed and the tenants' cattle was distrained and destroyed. In effect, the land had been enclosed against the tenants, for it was the custom in many manors that the common fields should be 'thrown open' for grazing on the stubble. The tenants' complaint was upheld, and the Crackenthorpes were bound over to keep the peace and to allow them to graze their cattle in the customary manner. Despite this, in 1528 James Crackenthorpe drove the cattle away from the common land and injured John Jackson, the keeper of the cattle, to the 'utter undoing' of the tenants.[70]

At Orton a dispute occurred which continued at least until 1535. John Warcop, a Clifford servant in a manor largely held by the Dacres, held a close of ten acres at Barbeck in Orton.[71] An undated Star Chamber case accused Lancelot Lowther and twenty-two others of entering the close, breaking down the bank, and destroying the trees. In 1535 Lancelot Lancaster, Lord Dacre's steward at Orton, led a large number of Dacre tenants to Smardale, where improvements made by Warcop were destroyed.[72] The accumulated animosity of local tenants towards Warcop's enclosures appears to have been directed into a riot which was one aspect of the Dacre offensive against the Earl of Cumberland and his allies.

Briscow, Crackenthorpe and Warcop were all Clifford men who were improving their land by enclosure. The example which they followed was that made by the Earl of Cumberland himself. A bailiffs' roll of 1542 indicates the amount which the Earl was spending on the repair and construction of enclosures in an ordinary year.[73]

> Paid to William Brunscale for making the hedge and wall at Newgate.   —   4s.   6d.
> Paid for upholding the hedge at Flakbrigg.   —   6s.   8d.
> **Paid for upholding the hedge about Whinfell Park.**
>   —   20s.
> For making posterns, locks and keys.   —   9s.   6d.
> Paid for making one rood of stone wall and 54 roods ditch.
>   —   23s.
> For making the new intake at Newgate.   —   25s.   11d.

[70] *Ibid.*, 31/44 amd 32/147.

[71] *Ibid.*, 28/124.

[72] *LP*, VIII, 1046.

[73] Joint Archives, Kendal, Account roll of Westmorland Estates, 1542.

Therefore in that year alone at least £4 9s. 7d. was spent on enclosing or maintaining existing enclosures on various parts of the Clifford estates in Westmorland. The same policy of enclosure was being pursued in the Yorkshire estates in Craven, and it was there that the first great protest against enclosure occurred. The Craven riots of 1535, which involved a number of tenants of the Abbey of Furness, were mainly directed against the Earl.[74] Of the eighty-two persons indicated, some forty were the Earl of Cumberland's own tenants, and these were only a small proportion of the hundreds of men, women and children who were involved. The remainder were tenants of John Lambert, another client of the Clifford house who had been making improvements by encroaching on the commons.

During the Pilgrimage of Grace the main riots against enclosures also took place on Clifford land, whence the complaint of the commons had originated. No specific instances are recorded for 1536, but in early January 1537 the Earl's new enclosures at Kirkby Stephen were torn down, and other parishes were instructed by the rebels to follow suit.[75] Enclosures at Brough were destroyed on 28 January. In a letter to the Lords of the Council the Duke of Norfolk reported these new riots, saying that 'people were never in the insurrection time more full of ill words than now'.[76] Later he attributed the new outbreaks to enclosures when he told Cromwell of 'the increasing of Lord's rents by inclosings'.[77] To this remark must be related a later one concerning the Earl's greed 'to get money of his tenants'.[78]

In fact, Norfolk's diagnosis of the problem loses some credibility when one remembers that no great enclosure disturbances occurred in 1536, and those of early 1537 were directly prompted by the actions of Thomas Clifford in trying to arrest two prominent rebel leaders at Kirkby Stephen. Just as the attacks on Briscow and Warcop incorporated a political element, so too did riots against the Earl of Cumberland's own enclosures. The background of rivalry with the Dacres, dislike of the Earl's policies by his tenants, and contempt of the Earl's inadequacy as warden of the march by the inhabitants of the region as a whole were all likely to produce rioting in hard times, and the interference of the Earl's bastard son made attacks on enclosures an obvious release of accumulated peasant anger.[79]

[74]*LP*, VIII, 863, 946, 970, 984, 991-3.

[75]*Ibid*., 687(2).

[76]*Ibid*., 319.

[77]*Ibid*., 478.

[78]*Ibid*., 919.

[79]See below, p. 122.

In most areas of the Lake Counties, enclosures presented no problem. Even in areas such as the Barony of Westmorland, where pressure on good land was greater, enclosures were not important enough to cause rebellion in their own right. Rather, they should be seen as a convenient objective for other aggressions, an outlet for rebellious spirits, and not a motive for rebellion. The contribution of enclosures to the Pilgrimage of Grace in the Lake Counties was small, in terms of both the areas involved and the intensity of emotion aroused.

Cornage

The rebel complaint against cornage was one of the least sophisticated of the commons' economic demands and reflected the grievance of a small interest group. The only written complaint was made in the letter from Musgrave and Pulleyn to Lord Darcy in which they demanded 'to have nowte gyelt and sarjeant corne laid down'.[80]

Neat geld or cornage was an ancient feudal tenure which was not restricted to the Lake Counties, but which had developed there in a particular way. Various suggestions have been made as to the origin of the tenure, the most prominent of which are that cornage was a cow-tax and that it was a form of grand serjeanty, the service of which was fulfilled by the winding of a horn at the first sign of invasion from the northern enemy.[81] More probably the original form of the word cornage was 'coronagium' or crown-rent. Only later did the tenure become linked with a *geldum animatum,* in this case neat geld, because payment was made in cattle rather than coin. As well as payment of money or cattle, the tenure demanded border service, and there can be little doubt that there was more to this than the winding of a horn. 'These cornage tenants were bound, in their most defensible array for the wars, to be ready to serve their Prince and the Lord of the Manor upon horseback or on foot, at their own proper costs and charges; and when the King's army passed into Scotland, they had the post of honour to march in the vanguard, and on their return in the rereguard.'[82]

Originally the whole of the counties of Cumberland and West-morland were subject to cornage when the land was parcelled out under Henry I. Later some areas transferred to other tenures. The

[80] PRO, S.P.1., III, p. 134, (*LP*, XI, 1080). See appendix.

[81] See Bouch and Jones, pp. 11-12. Also J. Nicholson and R. Burn; F. Pollock and T.W. Maitland, *History of English Law,* 2 vols (second edition, London, 1911); T.H.B. Graham, 'Cornage and Drengage', *CWAAS* new ser. 28 (1928); J.E.A. Jolliffe 'Northumbrian Institutions', *E.H.R.,* 12(1926).

[82] Nicholson and Burn, I, 18.

Barony of Kendal, for example, became the fee of one knight on payment of twenty marks. By the sixteenth century those areas which were still held by cornage found the tenure extremely beneficial to the sub-tenants, but not to the tenant-in-chief. The reasons for this were firstly that cornage exempted its holders from normal military service, and secondly that it provided tenants with security approaching that of freeholders.

The security of the tenure was founded on the peculiar method of transmission from the tenant-in-chief to the lesser tenants. Whereas the holder of a knight's fee took the responsibility for rendering service to the King and kept the military control and loyalty of his own tenants in his own hands, cornage demanded no military responsibilities to the tenant-in-chief. This has been summed up by saying that 'those peculiar services [that is, service on the borders] were rendered by others than territorial magnates, . . . the tenant in capite habitually compelled his under tenants to answer for a due proportion of the duty . . . In some cases, perhaps in all, the contributor to cornage rent was an under-tenant who had in effect become a tenant-in-chief because his superior lord had cast on him the duties of performing forinsec service to the King'.[83] Effectively, the tenant-in-chief had no authority over his tenants, whose tenure was thus closely akin to freehold. Estates and the payments made for them were hereditable and fixed. At the inception of the tenure payments had been apportioned within the Barony of Westmorland, firstly by the tenant-in-chief and then by the mesne tenants. Holders of relatively small pieces of land, such as a messuage and four acres of land at Crosthwaite, were effectively their own lords under the King. Whereas Thomas de Hellbeck paid threepence-halfpenny for his land in 1256, his descendants would have paid the same three hundred years later. The only change appears to have been the method of payment. Whereas the money was originally collected by the mesne tenant and passed on to the tenant-in-capite, by the sixteenth century the latter had appointed his own bailiffs to collect the money.

The income of the tenant-in-chief was thus unchanging. Between 1452 and 1527 no cornage rents were raised, and the income of the Earl of Cumberland from them was £27 9s. 8d.[84] This low yield of rents must have been irksome when one considers the profits of the mesne tenants, most of whom had apportioned out their land by tenures other than cornage. Lord Dacre, for example, held of the Earl of Cumberland Yanwath, Bolton, Brampton, Dufton, Hoff, Drybeck,

[83]Graham, p. 79.

[84]W. Ragg, 'The Feoffees of the Cliffords from 1283 to 1482', *CWAAS* new ser. 13 (1908).

and a moiety of the vast parish of Orton. For these he paid £2 3s. 9d., but his income from them in 1535 was £179 14s. 6d.[85] The Cliffords could only reclaim their land by direct purchase with the tenants' agreement — an unlikely contingency — or at the failure of a line. Other than the meagre rents, their only profit was from wardship, marriage and relief, payments which became due on the succession of a minor. These could be considerable, Hartley and Langton for example being worth £40 yearly. However, even these payments were irregular, and lack of evidence of them for the early sixteenth century indicates that they may have decayed.

The advantages to the tenant by cornage were thus considerable, and the power of the lord was at most nominal. Cornage payments in themselves offer no solution to the problem of rebel motivation in the Pilgrimage of Grace. However, it seems probable that associated payments were susceptible to exploitation, and it was against these that the rebels' anger was largely directed. In Westmorland the payment of puture of the serjeants, variously known as 'sarjeant corne', sergeant food, or bailiffs' oats, was made concurrently with cornage rent. In 1534 Clifford income from cornage and socage was £36 5s. 10½d. To this must be added a payment for sergeant food of £16 11s. 0½d. which was distributed amongst the wards of Westmorland as follows.[86]

Eastward	£9 11s. 9d.
Westward	£1 12s. 5d.
Middleward	£5 6s. 10½d.

Sergeant food was apportioned in proportion to cornage rents, and the burden therefore was carried by Eastward parish, the most vociferous during the Pilgrimage of Grace. Almost certainly these payments were made in kind. This would, of course, put a particular strain on the parishes in years of dearth and would thus have been intensified in such years, and a court case of the seventeenth century illustrates how bailiffs could exploit sergeant corn in time of dearth.[87] In 1629 the parishes of Shap, Hilton, Crosby Ravensworth and Smardale complained that Francis, Earl of Cumberland, had been collecting 'nowtgelt moneys' and sergeants oats to which he had no right. The charge had no foundation, but the court criticized the method of collection of the latter payment. The quantities of oats to be collected were stipulated, Shap paying 61 bushells, Smardale 15 bushells, and

[85]Department of Paelaeography and Diplomatic, Durham, C/201/3, Receivers Accounts.

[86]Manuscripts of his Grace the Duke of Devonshire at the Library, Chatsworth, Volume 10.

[87]Joint Archive, Kendal, Box 48.

Soulby 63 bushells. The complainants accused the Clifford bailiffs on five separate counts: of not spreading the payment but taking the whole burden for the parish from one individual: of distraining without notice if payment was not made on time: of accepting bribes from individuals who were ignored at the time of collection of the oats: of using large measures and only accepting highest quality oats: and of neglecting collections in years of plenty and demanding the accumulated total in years of dearth. Evidently the same type of exploitation was taking place on the estates held by cornage in Cumberland. The respective payments there were seawake and tournsilver, and where these or the cornage payment were witheld distraint was immediate. In 1616, for example, four oxen were removed from Uldale, a cow and a grey nag from Grinsdale, a nag from Beaumont, and a brown bay nag and a mare from Orton.[88]

No specific examples of exploitation of this type exist for the years preceding the Pilgrimage of Grace. However, in a situation where a harsh landlord was frustrated by the security of tenure of his tenants, he may have derived increased income from methods such as these.

The burden of extra payments may have motivated the men of Kirkby Stephen to complain about the tenure of cornage itself. The advantages of cornage to the sub-tenants have already been shown, and they would not have been abandoned lightly unless a better replacement could be found. There can be little doubt that the more desirable tenure, used already in some Westmorland and Cumberland parishes, was that of socage. It has been said of areas in which military tenures still existed that 'the time was already not far distant when those who held by the more honourable tenure of knight service would insist on its being assimilated to the humbler and less onerous tenure of the socager'.[89] Asby, Soulby, Warcop, Wharton and Tebay were amongst the parishes which paid only a quit-rent.[90] Of these, Asby paid the high sum of 26s. 8d., but Soulby and Warcop paid a total of one shilling and five pence, Wharton six shillings, and Tebay paid five shillings. The duties of the freeholder by socage were also far less than the burden placed on the cornage tenant. Possibly it was the contrast between cornage and socage which caused a dispute in Cumberland in 1532. In that year John Legh, who was canvassing Cromwell for the office of sheriff of Cumberland, wrote that 'the free-holders are put in such fear by those who claim the tenure of the cornage'.[91] Legh

---

[88]Joint Archive, Carlisle, D.Lec., a note of distraints for cornage, 1616.

[89]R.H. Tawney, p. 29.

[90]W. Ragg, 'Feoffees of the Cliffords', pp. 292-4.

[91]LP, V, 1447.

assured Cromwell that if he became sheriff he would maintain the King's rights with regard to his tenants. There can be no doubt that cornage had lapsed in that area, but was now seen to be more profitable to the landlord than the purer form of freehold.

The rebels of Westmorland, the only area from which complaint about cornage came in 1536, were therefore worried on two counts. Firstly, subsidiary payments were being demanded which undermined their security, especially in years of dearth. Secondly, and because of this, they wanted cornage and sergeant food 'layde down'.[92] Their unspoken desire was to have the tenure changed to socage.

However, it should be emphasised that this complaint came only from one community, that of Kirkby Stephen. Possibly, the chief influence was Robert Pulleyn, a signatory of the letter to Lord Darcy. Pulleyn's status as a freeholder by cornage is known from the fact that early in 1537 he 'had paid his neat geld and had put divers men in possession of lands and had taken many bribes'.[93] The men of Kirkby Stephen wanted to spoil his goods, but others spoke for him and they were restrained. In 1534 Pulleyn had made a substantial payment to the bailiff of the Earl of Cumberland for 'comensale', a sum of money contributed towards a feast day in medieval times.[94] This payment does not appear elsewhere on the Clifford bailiffs rolls, and Pulleyn was the only person to pay it. Possibly 'comensale' was in turn a subsidiary payment of sergeant corn. If the levy was placed on him by the bailiff, it would explain his personal involvement with the complaint against cornage, and its appearance amongst the economic demands of the rebels.

Certainly, concern about cornage did not intensify until the early seventeenth century, and it cannot be seen as a prominent grievance voiced during the Pilgrimage of Grace. It may have affected a few communities, or possibly only Kirkby Stephen or Robert Pulleyn himself. Cornage was not a major element in the rebellion of the Lake Counties of 1536, but quite possibly a minor grievance likely to be exacerbated in time of dearth.

Entry fines, tithes, enclosure and neat-geld were the four specific economic grievances voiced by the rebels of the Lake Counties. Possibly these complaints were made with greater force because of the effects of harvest failure in 1535 and 1536. Dearth, a cause of temporary economic pressure, added to the urgent need for a halt to

---

[92]PRO, S.P.1., 111, p. 134. (*LP*, XI, 1080).

[93]*LP*, XII(1), 687(2).

[94]The Library, Chatsworth, Volume 10.

the long-term changes which were threatening the livelihood of the inhabitants of the region. Even so, an examination of these four elements has shown that their contribution to the rebellion has been exaggerated. Certainly entry fines were a problem throughout the region, and those tenants who had not already suffered from inflated gressums were nevertheless threatened by them. Tithes, too, were a problem affecting the whole region, although only a few communities ·voiced their protest during the Pilgrimage of Grace. Neat geld was a complaint restricted to the town of Kirkby Stephen, and its appearance amongst the rebel articles is more an indication of the town's importance in the rebellion than of that of neat geld itself. Enclosures had threatened the livelihood of only a small number of communities in the region, and demonstrations against them were primarily political.

It would be wrong to say that no men joined the rebel ranks simply because of poverty or hunger. Economic changes were taking their toll on middling and poor peasants alike. Therefore one can assume that some of the rebels who attacked the tithe barns wanted the grain within and had no wider objectives. Similarly it seems very likely that a considerable number of people who joined the musters and took the rebel oath did so on the assumption that action would be taken against lords who had been raising entry fines, and that they were not very interested in other issues.

Had these been the sole, or even the main motives of the majority of rebels, the Pilgrimage of Grace in the Lake Counties would have taken the form which many historians have wrongly attributed to it — one of mob raids on the property of gentlemen and tithe barns, direct action to alleviate immediate hardship, riots on the pattern of the Craven riots of 1535. The fact that this was not the case, and that the rebels were disciplined, purposeful, united, and well led, must make the social and economic explanation of the rising inadequate. Probably the most significant contribution made towards the rebellion by economic hardship was that it created a general background of dissatisfaction which made people more willing to join a rising in which other issues also bulked large. For a full understanding of the origins and nature of the Pilgrimage of Grace it is necessary to turn to religious and political issues as well as economic and social ones.

Religious Grievances

The rebellion in the Lake Counties has often been considered a separate episode, disconnected from the Pilgrimage of Grace elsewhere because the complaints there were not primarily directed against the changes brought about by the Henrician Reformation.[95] A reconsideration of the religious standpoint of the rebels of the Lake Counties should prove that they were far more concerned with issues to do with the Reformation than has been acknowledged in the past.

It will be shown how the precipitants of the rising were concerned with religion. The theme which ran through all three of the messages from Yorkshire was the need to serve God and the Church. Inevitably, different localities added their own grievances to the manifesto, and often these grievances became more important. However, until the rebels dispersed from Broadfield Oak on 3 November a strong interest was maintained in the religious issues that concerned them. Often this interest was rather naive. For example, the captains of Penrith commanded all men to live in peace and say 'Five aves, five paters and a creed', while at the same time the chaplains of poverty were instructed to give teaching in the faith to all men on pain of death.[96] The 'captains' mass', perhaps the most famous incident to take place in the Lake Counties during the Pilgrimage of Grace, displays a similar irony. The four captains of Penrith, Thomas Burtbeck, Gilbert Whepdale, John Beck and Robert Mounsey, with swords drawn followed the vicar of Brough into Penrith church. Swords were then put up, and the vicar said mass and gave one of the Ten Commandments, the breaking of which was said to be the cause of the trouble. This symbolic ritual was repeated until one of the priests suggested that naked swords should not be brought into church, and as a consequence the ceremony was discontinued.

Several separate religious issues troubled the rebels of the Lake Counties. Some of these were shared with the Pilgrims in Yorkshire, and others appear to have been particular local problems. A significant underlying cause of discontent was the rumour circulating throughout the north in 1536 and stimulating fear amongst the commons about forthcoming religious changes. Three rumours were common to the counties involved in the Pilgrimage of Grace: that all jewels and vessels of the parish churches were to be taken away and replaced with base metals; that parish churches were to be five miles apart and, where they were nearer, superfluous churches were to be pulled down and parishes united; and that for every christening, marriage or burial a tribute had to be paid to the King.[97] Instances of each rumour can be found in the Lake Counties. At Dent a blacksmith

---

[95] Some interpretations of this nature are dealt with in the Introduction, p. 2.

[96] *LP.* XII(1). 687(2).

[97] Dodds, pp. 76-7.

told William Breyar that the King was a thief, 'for he pulleth down all our churches in the country'.[98] The people of Dent were sworn to an oath 'to suffer no spoils nor suppressions of abbeys, parish churches, or their jewels and to pay no more money'. At Hawkshead it was stated amongst several 'naughty articles' that no infant should receive the blessed sacrament of baptism unless a tribute was paid to the King.[99] Similar rumours were voiced by William Barret, a tanner from Craven. He was arrested in Manchester for saying that the Duke of Norfolk, on arrival in Yorkshire, would 'either have of every plough 6s. 8d. or take an ox of every one that would not pay, and that every christening and burying should pay 6s. 8d.'.[100] Barret had been amongst the rebels at Carlisle, and it can be assumed that these rumours were voiced there too. He was hanged in chains at Manchester.

One origin of one of these rumours was the suppression of the smaller abbeys. The monasteries threatened by the dissolution act of 1536 were those worth less than two hundred pounds. Nine institutions of the Lake Counties were so classified, although Shap was exempted and played no part in the rebellion, but for the use of the church door as a posting place for rebel bills. Of the remaining eight institutions five do not appear in the documentation of the rebellion. These were the priories of Armathwaite, Seaton, Wetheral and St Bees and the Abbey of Calder. Lanercost Priory was mentioned in the King's correspondence as a place which gave resistance, presumably against the King's officers, but no details have survived. The remaining two, Cartmel and Cornishead, do appear to have been enthusiastically supported by the rebels in the Lake Counties and not simply because their tenants, feared a change of landlord.[101] Their representatives in York were able to gain permission for the canons to re-enter their houses. Some part in the rebellion was also played by the monks of the larger houses at Furness, Holm Cultram and Carlisle who identified themselves with the rebellion. This identification was reciprocated in some parts of the region. The men of Westmorland and north Lancashire, and particularly their leader William Collins, seem to have wanted the monasteries to survive. At Hawkshead the call to rebellion summoned men to join the ranks of those who go forth 'openly for the aid and assistance of your holy church and for the

[98] *LP.* XI. 841.

[99] *Ibid.,* 892.

[100] *Ibid.,* XII(1), 520, 632.

[101] Haigh, *Lancashire Monasteries,* Chapter VI, provides a detailed account of the part played by these institutions in the rebellion and Haigh, *Reformation and Resistance,* p. 119, comments further on the suppression of the North Lancashire monasteries.

reformation of such abbeys and monasteries not dissolved and suppressed without any just cause'.[102] The priory at Cartmel was supported by its tenants, ten of whom were hanged for their part in a small uprising after the King's pardon had been read.

Generally speaking, however, the religious zeal of the inhabitants of the Lake Counties was not directed towards the defence of the monasteries. The vicarious enthusiasm of the Abbot of Holm does not seem to have communicated itself to the rebels of Cumberland, for despite the fact that he represented the rebels at Carlisle, his followers were unwilling to obey his command to join in the February insurrection. At Furness the tenants appear to have been pressed into service. Several of them escaped recruitment, and after the rebellion there was no shortage of people willing to testify against the abbey. This, the most powerful house in the region expressed views which were of little interest to the rebels; the Abbey was not yet threatened with dissolution; and apart from the tenants who may already have been alienated by its economic policies, Furness was too isolated to expect mass support. The fact that the monasteries of the Lake Counties were sparsely spread across the region and distant from the chief centres of rebellion made them irrelevant to the rebels, and while help from the brethren was no doubt gladly accepted, their preservation was not high on the list of rebel priorities.

Neither was the question of the royal supremacy over the Church an important issue in the Lake Counties although it was severely criticised by the monks of Furness. Henry Salley, one of the monks who was later imprisoned at Lancaster, stated that the world was never good since 'secular men and knaves had rule upon us and the King made head of the church'.[103] Another monk, John Broughton, said that the Bishop of Rome was unjustly put down, but that all would be put right again within three years. The attack on the supremacy at Furness also took the form of a criticism of the King himself. At root this was a resentment of interference with the internal affairs of the abbey, and John Green stated that in future the King would not choose their abbot, but they would choose their own. However, the attack was made on broader issues as well. One monk of Furness was heard to say that the King had no right to the crown as his father had taken it by the sword. Several of the brethren including John Harrington and John Broughton made a prophecy that 'in England shall be slain the decorat rose in his mother's belly', another version of which was that 'the red rose should die in his mother's womb'. This

[102]*Ibid.*, XI, 892(2).

[103]This and the following statements from Furness are calendared in *LP*, XII(1), 841 (1, 2 and 3).

was interpreted to mean that the King should die at the hands of priests, who were the servants of the King's mother, the Church.

However, the attitude of the monks of Furness was the most forthright criticism of the King and perhaps the most direct statement against the supremacy; elsewhere the rebels tried to veil their dissatisfaction with a statement of loyalty towards Henry VIII. In the initial stages of the rebellion both Kendal and Penrith took oaths that identified them with the defence of the King's honour. A statement issued in Lancashire under the name of 'Master Poverty, the conductor protector and maintainer of the whole commonality' proclaimed that 'they intend the defence of the faith of Christ by license of Henry VIII who, though styled Defender of the Faith, yet by certain heretics of the time they see it confounded, not ashaming in open preaching to blaspheme the honour of God by spoiling and suppressing holy places, as abbeys, churches, and ministers of the same, and despising the laws of the Holy Mother Church; blaspheming also our lady and other saints days'.[104] That this was not intended to be a direct criticism of the King can be seen from the conclusions: 'and ever God save the King and send him good council.' The Ballad on the Pilgrimage of Grace, written by one of the brethren at Sawley Abbey, makes quite clear where the fault was thought to lie. The final verse attacks Cromwell, Cranmer, Rich, and in all probability Latimer, Leyton and Legh.

> Crim, crame, and riche
> with three ell and the liche
> As sum men teache
> God them amend!
> And that Aske may,
> Without delay,
> Here make a stay
> And well to end![105]

While the rebels seem to have borne a genuine dislike of Cromwell, the attack on him served another purpose. It provided the rebels throughout the north with a scapegoat and enabled them to equate their insurrection with loyalty to the King. The Lancashire rebels announced their intention 'to expulse all villain blood from the Kings Grace and his privy council for the commonwealth and the restoring of Christ's church'.[106] In Dent, when William Breyar arrived in the King's livery and the blacksmith called Henry VIII a thief, another villager rebuked him, saying that 'it is not the King's deed, but

[104]*Ibid.*, XI, 892(1).

[105]Quoted fully in *E.H.R.* 5 (1890), 331.

[106]*LP,* XI, 892(2).

the deed of Cromwell, and if we had him here we would crum him and crum him that he was never so crummed, and if thy master was here we would new crown him'.[107] Complaints against the standards of the secular clergy were also directed against Cromwell. Musgrave and Pulleyn, in their letter to Lord Darcy expressed a wish 'to put in their room to serve God others that would be glad to keep hospitality, for some of them are no priests that have the benefice in hand, and some are Lord Cromwell's chaplains'.[108] During the rebellion such benefices and beneficed men were seized for the maintenance of the rebels, as in the case of Parson Threlkeld of Melmerby.[109]

The rebels of the Lake Counties in this way attempted to gloss over the contradiction of expressing loyalty to the King and attacking the royal supremacy at the same time. Outside the Furness area such attacks were confined to prayers for the Pope. At Kendal three hundred people threatened to throw the curate into the river if he would not proclaim the Pope to be head of the church. Later, the second curate, Walter Browne, resolved the dispute by praying for the Pope and cardinals. At Brough the vicar, Robert Thompson, experienced similar threats after the calling of the pardon.[110] He was commanded by Christopher Blenkinsop, Thomas Taylor, and Matthew Wharton to pray for the Pope. By his own confession 'for fear of his life' Thompson commanded all to pray for the King as head of the church and for the Bishop of Rome and cardinals.

If the rebels achieved an uneasy compromise with regard to the supremacy, they were committed in their opposition to changes in church ceremony. The commons of the Lake Counties were deeply troubled by their priests' interpretations of the Ten Articles of 1536, and in particular their complaints concerned the bidding of beads and calling of saints' days.[111] The first rising at Kirkby Stephen was started when the priest omitted the calling of the holyday of St Luke.[112] Probably he had also changed the form of beads bidding (that is, the telling of the rosary) for when Robert Pulleyn returned from the conference at Doncaster he proclaimed that 'priests should bid holidays and beads as before'.[113] Unless this was a fabrication by

[107]*LP*, XI, 841.

[108]*Ibid.*, 1080.

[109]See below, p. 96.

[110]*LP*, XII(1), 384, and *ibid.*, 637(2).

[111]K. Thomas, *Religion and the Decline of Magic*, chapter 1, substantiates the idea that such aspects of religion as prayers and saints' days were of great significance to ordinary people.

[112]*LP*, XII(1), 637(2).

[113]*Ibid.*, 687(2).

Pulleyn, it seems likely that he had made an interim settlement similar to that which had been made permitting the monks to reenter their houses pending the decision of a northern parliament.[114] At Kendal, the bidding of beads was also considered important, and when the threat was made against the curate there, the fact that he had not bid beads in the old way was as much a cause of the trouble as the supremacy.[115]

An attack on beads bidding is not explicit in the Ten Articles, and does not appear to have been so until 1559, when the Injunctions forbade works 'devised by man's fantasies' such as praying on beads.[116] Traditional rites and ceremonies were in fact permitted by the articles of 1536, insofar as they were 'honest and commendable'. Evidently the northern clerics thought that certain aspects of beads bidding were not, for changes were made at both Kirkby Stephen and Kendal.[117] Firstly, praying for the Pope was removed from the round. Secondly, anything which was seen to be controversial, such as praying for particular saints, had become dangerous and may also have been omitted. Thirdly, the Injunctions of the summer of 1536 commanded that the Pater Noster, the Articles, and the ten commandments should be recited in the mother tongue.[118] That part of beads bidding which was concerned with reciting the Pater was thus transformed just before the outbreak of rebellion, and possibly the abandoning of the traditional Latin was the offence which caused the men of Kendal to demand bidding of beads 'in the old way'.[119] There can be little doubt that interference with this ceremony was particularly abominable to people in such areas as the Lake Counties. Even after the Injunctions of 1559 'a persistent use of the rosary must have continued amongst the country people in remote places . . . because the rosary was one of the most common forms of devotion'.[120] In opposing changes in the ritual, the people of Kirkby Stephen and Kendal were defending that part of a service which was familiar to them and the main part of a service in which they could actually become involved. Although the government's attack on the rosary had only just begun, they were anticipating a much later demand by

[114]See below, p. 116.

[115]*LP.* XII(1). 384.

[116]H. Gee & W.J. Hardy, *Documents Illustrative of English Church History,* pp. 419-20.

[117]*LP.* XII(1). 687(2): 914.

[118]Gee and Hardy. p. 272.

[119]*LP.* XII(1). 914.

[120]D. Horton-Davies. *Worship and Theology in England. From Cranmer to Hooker, 1534-1603,* p. 154.

the Western Rebels of 1549 to return to the tradition of bidding beads.[121] Thus it was that, at rebel musters, the Vicar of Brough commanded that the commons should live in peace and say 'five paters, and a creed'.[122]

The attack on the adoration of saints was a more definite aspect of the Ten Articles. The seventh article confirmed that saints should be honoured. The eighth article provided that, despite this, grace, remission of sin and salvation could be obtained only from God by the mediation of 'Our Saviour Christ'. Saints could only be intercessors, and the honouring of them should be done without any superstition that 'any saint is more merciful, or will hear us sooner than Christ'.[123] Holy days were still to be celebrated 'except they be mitigated and moderated by the commandment of us, the supreme head, to the ordinaries'.[124] In fact the reductions in numbers of holy days, as decreed in July 1536, were severe. At harvest time only the feasts of the Apostles, the Virgin Mary and St George were to be observed. During the law terms holy days were restricted to the observance of the Nativity of St John the Baptist, Ascension day, All Hallows and Candlemas. All feasts of dedication were to be observed on the first Sunday in October, and church holy days only if the feast fell on an authorised saint's day.

The omission of time-honoured saints' days was thus a contributory element in the rebellion. At Watton in Yorkshire the omission of the calling of St Wilfrid's day caused stirrings amongst the people.[125] At Kirkby Stephen it was the omission of the calling of St Luke's day which prompted the people to rise.[126] The significance of St Luke to the people of Kirkby Stephen is hard to find. It is possible that he was important to agricultural communities. Becon, when mocking the devotion of the humble Roman Catholic towards saints, imagined them saying; 'If we fast the blessed saints' evens and worship them with a Paternoster, Ave and Creed, they will do for us whatever we ask. St George will defend us in battle against our enemies. St Barbara will keep us from thundering and lightening . . . St Luke will save our ox.'[127] Possibly the importance of St Luke in the New Testament

[121]*Ibid.*, p. 130.

[122]*LP*, XII(1), 687(2).

[123]Printed in full in C. Hardwick, *A History of the Articles of Religion (London, 1888)*, Appendix I, pp. 237-258.

[124]*Ibid.*

[125]Dodds, I, 152-3.

[126]*LP*, XII(1), 687(2). See below, p. 91

[127]Quoted in Horton-Davies, p. 20.

recommended him to the rebels; later, his importance was to be recognised even by the protestant Church which has given him a status rivalling that of the apostles. A more simple explanation is that the omission of the calling of St. Luke's day was the last straw and sparked off rebellion. The liturgical changes brought about by the Ten Articles would have meant little to the commons of the Lake Counties. Where changes did affect them, such as in beads bidding and the observance of saints' days, they saw good reason to protest. They were hardly likely to have been fighting against the introduction of the thin end of the protestant wedge. Rather, they were simply defending what they had always known and accepted.

Any assumption that the influence of religion in the Lake Counties was 'negligible' is patently false. Part of the reason for this misconception lies in the fact that historians have looked beyond the obvious. One distinguished historian of the Reformation has classified the religious motives of the rebels into three: the defence of the monasteries, dislike of doctrinal heresy, and rejection of the royal supremacy.[128] With the exception of the men of Kendal and the southwest of the region the rebels of the Lake Counties were lacking in sympathy with the monasteries, they were unaware of the academic complications of doctrinal heresy, and complaints against the royal supremacy were restricted to monks and, as far as we know, small communities such as Dent. What the commons were protesting about was much simpler than any of these things. They saw changes taking place in traditional services and customs which were not to their liking, and rumour, misleadingly substantiated by such events as the closure of the smaller monasteries indicated that worse was to come. It was for these reasons that the rebels followed the cross at their musters and enforced the continuance of the religious traditions which they sought to defend. Moreover, while the regular and secular clergy played a part in this, the initiative came as much from the commons when leadership from the clergy was lacking.

Political Grievances

If religious and economic issues were at stake in the Pilgrimage of Grace in the Lake Counties, so too were political ones. Two distinct political elements in the rebellion which were unique to the Lake Counties can be identified as vital issues in the events of the disturbed months. Firstly, the family feud between Cliffords and Dacres continued during the rebellion, and secondly, the weakness of the Earl of Cumberland's wardenship and the consequent dangers of Scots raiding provided the commons with a major grievance.

[128]Dickens, 'Secular and Religious Motivation', p. 57.

It has been suggested that the forces of law and order had been neutralised by the dispute between Clifford and Dacre which had taken place in the years preceding the rebellion. After the trial of 1534 Lord Dacre had pursued a policy of aggression against the Cliffords which not only encouraged law-breaking but also undermined the already weak wardenship of the Earl of Cumberland. Once the rebellion was under way the gentlemen of the Lake Counties, confused and leaderless, found themselves fleeing from the rebel musters or being forced to take an oath to the rebels' cause. Those gentlemen who were forced to attend musters suffered the further humiliation of playing a passive role at the command of peasant representatives, a situation which in normal circumstances would have been unthinkable for men of their station.

William Lord Dacre was the one figure capable of organising the gentlemen and commanding a large enough force to challenge the rebels. However, throughout the Pilgrimage of Grace he played an uncommitted role which suggests more than one interpretation. Lord Dacre became aware of the outbreak of rebellion on 10 October.[129] He remained in the Cumberland area for at least a month, taking a defensive position at Naworth Castle. Perhaps he thought that he had something to fear from the rebels, for on 30 October he sent a servant, John Skelton, to Carlisle with a proposition for Henry Lord Clifford.[130] Dacre offered to render assistance at Carlisle in the event of a siege there if Clifford would reciprocate for Naworth. Subsequently the bargain proved hollow, for in early November Dacre left the region for an uncertain destination, but probably the site of the modern Castle Howard in Yorkshire.[131] Thereafter certain events occurred which indicate the continuation of the old feud with the Cliffords and connections with the Pilgrimage of Grace. In fact Dacre appears to have pursued the policy of redressing his grievances under the cover of rebellion. It has been shown that during 1536 attacks took place on Clifford servants, and it is possible that these incidents occurred during the rebellion.[132] Certainly Dacre tenants adopted their lord's cause, and Sir Thomas Wharton was one person who was sought out so that 'for old displeasures between him and Lord Dacres he should die'.[133] Wharton was never captured, but in a later incident another Dacre enemy, Sir William Musgrave, almost lost his life. On 9

[129]*LP*, XI, 647.

[130]*Ibid.*, 1331.

[131]*Ibid.*, 1096.

[132]See above, pp. 36-8.

[133]*LP*, XI, 1046(3).

December Richard Dacre, son to Lord William, met Henry Lord Clifford in the church door at Carlisle

> and looked upon him with a haughty and proud countenance, not moving his bonnet; and after going out of the churchyard chanced to meet with Sir William Musgrave, and without speaking any word plucked out his dagger and took him by the shoulder, and would have slain him in case he had not leaped back from him and plucked out his dagger, and that one of the sons of Lord Fetherstanhaugh had not with his dagger drawn leaped betwixt them.[134]

Richard Dacre then went to the market place, and with the words 'A Dacre! A Dacre!' assembled a company of followers. Aglionby, the mayor, commanded him to leave the market place, but he refused to do so until the officials called the town to harness against him. Richard Dacre then went to his lodgings, dined, and left the town only to return the next day. Lord Clifford was waiting for him, and with a body of men forced him to leave. Richard Dacre was not only connected in this way with the family feud against Cliffords and their associates, but was also linked with the rebel movement. On 15 November, the occasion of the muster at Broadfield Oak which followed the declaration of the truce, Richard adopted the title 'Grand Captain' and made Christopher Lee, a kinsman and servant, his deputy.[135]

In all probability this positive connection with the rebels was not Dacre policy. In the absence of William Lord Dacre, Sir Christopher Dacre, the much respected uncle of Lord William, became the most prominent figure in Cumberland. He intervened only once during the first rebellion, and on that occasion was largely responsible for persuading the rebels to disperse from the first Broadfield Oak muster of 3 November.[136] They disbanded for ten days, by which time the news of the truce was accepted as genuine. Richard Dacre's later adoption of the rebel cause was thus belated and insignificant, and possibly he was acting entirely independently from family policy.

However, if one accepts that the Dacres did pursue their traditional feud with the Cliffords but that they remained neutral or at most passively loyal during the rebellion, still their behaviour had important consequences. Thomas Cromwell was probably correct in his diagnosis of William Lord Dacre's behaviour.[137] Before he left the region the Dacre tenants were restrained, and those who had taken the

[134]*Ibid.*, 1331.

[135]*Ibid.*,

[136]*LP*, XII(1), 687(1).

[137]*Ibid.*, XI, 1331.

rebel oath must have been aware of the danger which was threatened by a potentially loyal Lord Dacre. His departure was not only taken as a signal by his own tenants to join the rebellion, but also provided other rebels with the security of knowing that swift retribution was unlikely to descend upon them from Naworth. It is likely that Dacre was strong enough to be able, had he desired, to turn the rebellion in the Lake Counties into a potent force. This he did not do, but conversely his presence as a servant of the King might have been enough to curb the rebellion. His absence, and the unleashing of his veteran tenants, was a negative political factor which had severe consequences for the rebel movement.

The pursuit of the Dacre-Clifford feud and the absence of restraint contributed considerably to the course of the rising, but more important than either of these factors was the situation of the Earl of Cumberland, warden of the march.

Certainly the Earl faced many disadvantages as warden which were beyond his control, Dacre opposition being a prime factor. But even accepting this it must be admitted that his performance during the rebellion was unimpressive. On hearing of the rising on 16 October the Earl left Skipton for Carlisle, but when on the following day he was confronted by a rebel force he returned to the safety of Skipton castle.[138] The story of the unsuccessful siege that followed has been amply related elsewhere.[139] Clifford enemies from throughout the north joined the besiegers who concocted various unpleasant schemes to draw the Earl from his shelter. Without full-scale siege machinery they had in fact little chance of success. When Sir William Musgrave arrived at Skipton during the uneasy weeks following the truce he found the Earl 'so well victualled and furnished that he cares little for the malice of his enemies'.[140] The Earl was comfortable, and the only effect of the siege (which he made no attempt to break) was to render him impotent in the execution of his wardenship.

This impotence was recognised by the rebels in the Lake Counties and was seen by them as a considerable danger. In the past, the warden of the march had been responsible for organising defences against the Scots, and the Dacres had executed this aspect of the office with considerable competence. Now the warden was virtually an absentee, a man unfamiliar with the border, and quite incapable of meeting the demands of his office. Furthermore, the traditional

---

[138]*Ibid.*, XI, 927.

[139]Dodds, I, 208-9, and James, 'First Earl of Cumberland', p. 47.

[140]*LP*, XI, 1228.

bastion against the Scots, Carlisle, was being held by the Earl of Cumberland's son, who would not surrender the city to the rebels. In October 1536 Henry Lord Clifford had been travelling to Berwick when he was spotted by rebels, who chased him to Carlisle where he lay hidden for four days.[141] According to the Earl, the townsmen would have submitted to the rebels but for the influence of his son who appeared amongst them saying 'he would stand as my deputy their captain and jeopardy his life with them'.

The knowledge of Carlisle's hostility to and dislike of the Cliffords were important factors in the rebels' behaviour, but they also realised the need to take Carlisle not as a defence against the King, but against the Scots. The rebels' fear of Scots raiders was evident throughout the rebellion. Part of the proclamation made at every muster stated that

> because the rulers of this country do not ride among us and defend us from the robbing of the thieves and Scots that . . . iiii capitaynes be chosen which are called charity faith poverty and pity which command you to . . . be ready one to help another. And follow the skaw [warden?] when the thieves or Scots wold rob or invade us either by night or day.[142]

The men of Kirkby Stephen demanded that, having taken the rebel oath and restored the abbeys, they should show 'such demeanor towards the Scot that no parade of war might ensure but all to be kept in good quiet and peace'.[143] The rebels' fears were heightened by the news that Carlisle was standing firm against them and that raids were already taking place from across the border: 'for Aske and Levyn and the black quarters wold rob and destroy them, so that no man might take their rest in the night nor ride safely in the day. For word came to them the same day that divers men's goods dwelling about Carlisle were driven away'.[144] This news, brought to the muster at Sandale hill on Friday 27 October, was followed by the immediate granting of permission for men living near Carlisle to go home to defend their property.

Two main reasons can be identified for the appearance of such fears at the time of the rebellion. The first concerned the deteriorating relationships between England and Scotland during the autumn and winter of 1536 to 1537. At this time James V of Scotland was preparing for a marriage with Madeleine, daughter to Francis I of

[141]*Ibid.*, XI, 927.
[142]PRO, S.P.1, 117, pp. 46-69. (*LP*, XII(1), 687(2)).
[143]*Ibid.*
[144]*Ibid.*

France.[145] James spent December 1536 near Paris and was married on New Year's Day 1537. Henry VIII strongly disapproved of the French marriage, not least because he had not been consulted. When the French Ambassador requested that James should be allowed to return home through England, Henry replied that 'the King's honour is not to receive the King of Scots into his realm unless he will come as his Grace's vassal'.[146] Rejection of his request and careful soliciting from Rome turned James towards an alliance, ultimately with both France and Spain, against England. In fact, this contingency was unlikely, for the Emperor and Francis were already at war and the Spanish inclined towards friendship with England. However, the threat of a Catholic alliance was ever-present, and the return of James by sea to his home might signal the outbreak of war. The Scots themselves appear to have been favourable to a renewal of hostilities. They disliked Henry VIII and his policies, and if they were to strike at England the rebellion there offered them an excellent opportunity to fight from a position of advantage.[147] Henry's awareness of this is reflected in his concern to reinforce the dilapidated border strongholds at Carlisle and Bewcastle after the defeat of the rebels. However, this was only precautionary. Henry was probably aware that James would not fight without Francis and that the French were already involved in hostilities with Spain. His refusal to allow James's passage through England should therefore not be seen as a throwing down of the English gauntlet, but more as a straightforward diplomatic rebuff in return for James's lack of consultation. Henry's security was also reinforced by James's delay in sailing from Rouen, the new Queen being consumptive and unsuited to a winter voyage. Thus, for the time being, the crisis passed.

Henry was not a man to lose the opportunity which the international situation provided to exploit a rebel weakness. In late October, when he was drafting a pardon for the rebels, he reproached them for their insurrection which was to the 'advancement of our ancient enemies the Scots'.[148] Ellerker and Bowes, on their return to the rebels from Henry's court, were instructed to declare that 'his Majesty takes it unkindly that they should thus assemble, leaving their natural country, their wives, children and households behind them for a prey to their ancient and deadly enemies the Scots, who, the King is informed, are preparing upon the occasion of their insurrection to

[145]Dodds, II. 240.

[146]Ibid., p. 241.

[147]For example see Dodds, II. 244.

[148]LP, XI. 955.

execute their malice upon them unless the King provides for their defence'.[149] Rumours circulated of the gathering of Scotsmen on the border. At both Newark and Pontefract it was reported that twenty thousand Scots were mustering.

There was no possibility of the rebels making an alliance with the Scots. Even Lord Darcy, one of the nobles connected with Chapuys' conspiracy to organise a rising of the northern Catholic nobility, stated that he was ready to lead thirty thousand men against Scotland.[150] The men of the Lake Counties were similarly hostile to their northern neighbours. Raiding across the border was, after all, a seasonal occupation for the men of north Cumberland. They were ready to defend England against the Scots but had no faith in the Earl of Cumberland, the man appointed to lead them on the King's behalf, for their criticism of the 'rulers of this country' who 'did not ride among us and defend us' was directed at him. The rebels' solution was to elect their own leaders and to attempt to secure the vitally important city of Carlisle for the rebellion.

In the wider context of relationships between lord and tenant, what was taking place is extremely significant. It has been suggested that the men of Cumberland and Westmorland whose aim was 'to put an end to gentlemen' were in the vanguard of class war.[151] Certainly there were gentlemen who were very unpopular, such as John Legh and Peter Middleton, and they became the prime targets for the rebels of particular communities. However, the movement as a whole was much more in 'the old spirit' than the new.[152] The widespread support given to the initially hesitant and subsequently unwilling Dacre, and the deferential letter to the much respected Lord Darcy both hark back to a feudal relationship between lord and peasant.[153] This can be explained by the fact that the defence of the border was more important to many rebels than the struggle against those gentlemen who were raising entry fines. In recent months the border problem had been increased by the ineptitude of the Earl of Cumberland, and by his policies which were undermining traditional patterns of border clientage. Furthermore, there was the immediate problem of Carlisle. The rebels considered that control of the town and castle was essential for defence against the Scots, and ironically it was being held against

[149]*Ibid.*, 1064.

[150]*Ibid.*, 1086.

[151]See above, p. 2.

[152]Tawney, p. 322.

[153]Such an interpretation is peculiar to the Lake Counties, and provides an interesting contrast with recent assessments of the nature of the wider Pilgrimage of Grace, such as that in G. R. Elton, *Reform and Reformation* (London, 1977) pp. 266-70.

them by Lord Clifford, son of the man whose failures had inspired the commons' fears in the first place. Greater irony still lies in the fact that this feudal element of the rebellion was being led from below in an attempt to re-establish the traditional pattern of military relationships. When Lord Dacre failed to reciprocate the rebels' confidence in him, the commons nevertheless continued to pursue his cause against the Cliffords, and arranged their own system for the maintenance of border defence.

This aspect of the rebellion could hardly feature amongst any official articles of complaint, but there can be little doubt that the political struggles in the Lake Counties and the border problem were prominent features of the rising, especially in the northern part of the region.

5

THE REBELLION

Precipitants

Controversy still surrounds the problem of the immediate origins of the Pilgrimage of Grace. It is possible, for example, that the rising was planned in advance, in which case spontaneity need not be looked for in the events of October 1536.[1] However, if the Pilgrimage of Grace was planned, it is evident that an unfortunate coincidence caused a premature rebellion in Lincolnshire, which in turn acted as the precipitant for other regions before they were ready. This coincidence took the form of the three sets of commissioners who were at work in Lincolnshire in early October. One group was instituting the dissolution of the smaller monasteries; the second was enquiring into the condition of the Lincolnshire clergy; the third was assessing and collecting the subsidy. At the same time rumour in the north was rife, and the presence of the commissioners undoubtedly confirmed in the minds of many people that the rumours they had been hearing were well-founded.

The product of the fear which had been germinating in the minds of the men of Louth, and especially the prospect of the destruction of their church at the hands of the King's commissioners, was the rising which erupted on 2 October. Under the leadership of 'Captain Cobbler' the men of Louth seized the commissioner responsible for examining the clergy and then marched to take those responsible for the dissolution. On 3 October the commissioners for the subsidy fled from an advancing mob of 3,000 rebels. A mob they certainly were. No individual had the authority to control them, and Dr Raynes the notorious Chancellor to the Bishop of Lincoln was murdered with staves.

Enthusiasm for the uprising was great. By 5 October 10,000 rebels marched on Lincoln, and prepared a statement of grievances. However, cracks in the rebel façade were already beginning to show, primarily in disagreements between gentlemen and commons. On 10 October, when faced with the choice of going forward against a King's army or backing down, the gentlemen chose the latter course. Leaderless, the commons dispersed and the 'sordid' Lincolnshire

---

[1] The question of spontaneity in the West Riding of Yorkshire, and with broader implications for other regions, is dealt with in R.B. Smith, Chapter V, and in G.R. Elton, *Reform and Reformation*, pp. 264-71.

rising was over.[2] However, it had not been without effect. Whether Yorkshire was ready for rebellion or not, the rising in Lincolnshire acted as a precipitant, and by the time that the rising to the south of the Humber was dying, that to the north was enthusiastically getting under way.

The figure most associated with the Pilgrimage of Grace is Robert Aske, a gentleman of Yorkshire.[3] He was involved with the rebellion from the moment on 4 October when he was taken and sworn to the rebel cause while crossing the Humber into Yorkshire. Initially he used his influence to try to keep Yorkshire from rising — possibly to avoid involvement hoping that Lincolnshire alone could be successful. He was unable to provide the necessary restraint, and so by 10 October Aske was leading the Pilgrims of the East Riding. Three days later they marched on York, which was taken on 16 October. Here a proclamation was made.

> For this pilgrimage we have taken it for the preservation of Christ's Church, of this realm of England, the King our sovereign lord, the nobility and commons of the same, and to the intent to make petition to the King's highness for the reformation of that which is amiss within this his realm.[4]

The capture of York was a great triumph for the Pilgrims, and must have brought with it the support of many people who were waiting for firm evidence of the strength of the movement. Even before York had opened its gates, the news of the rebellion had been spreading to the north and west, and it was on 16 October that the Lake Counties first learned from Yorkshire correspondents that the Pilgrimage of Grace was taking place, and that the men of Cumberland, Westmorland and Lancashire were expected to take a part in it.[5]

This news alone may have been enough to turn the potentially rebellious inhabitants of the Lake Counties into a coherent rebel force. However, another precipitant can be identified which certainly would have provoked widespread disturbances in the north-west, even had the Pilgrimage of Grace not occurred. This was the disastrous harvest failure of autumn 1536.

It has been suggested that, had the rebellion derived primarily from

[2]For an account of the Lincolnshire rising, see M.E. James, 'Obedience and Dissent in Henrician England: The Lincolnshire Rebellion, 1536', *Past and Present*, No.48, 1970.

[3]The account of the part played in the rebellion by Aske as told in his own confession is printed in *E.H.R.*, 5 (1890), 550-73. The problem of Aske's role in the rebellion is still far from settled.

[4]*LP*, XI, 705.

[5]*Ibid.*, XII(1), 687(2).

economic motives, it would have taken place in 1535.[6] In that year grain was in short supply, and John Lambert, an associate of the Earl of Cumberland, wrote that 'the price of corn is daily enhanced'.[7] Many riots did occur, but there was no tie to link communities together. Enclosures were thrown down in Westmorland, but disturbances were localised, and there was neither the stimulus nor the opportunity for the rioters there to join forces with a larger movement with similar grievances in Craven.[8]

Harvests in 1536 were average for the country as a whole, but for a second year the Lake Counties were hit by dearth, and conditions must have become intolerable. An analysis of grain prices for the years 1534-7 (Table 4) shows why the effects of dearth were uncomfortable in 1535, and disastrous in 1536.[9] Using a price index which takes the years 1450-99 as the base figure, prices fluctuated as follows:

Table 4: Grain prices, 1534-7

(i)			
	Wheat	*Barley*	*Rye*	*Oats*
1534-5	116	106	225	145
1535-6	213	199	303	184
1536-7	156	124	154	182

(ii)			
1534-5 to 1535-6	84% rise	88% rise	34% rise	27% rise
1535-6 to 1536-7	27% fall	38% fall	49% fall	1% fall

The usefulness of these statistics is limited by the fact that they apply to the country as a whole, and that the most relevant ones, those for oats, come from Cambridge accounts. Even so, a comparison of relative prices shows that oats prices, the most important for Westmorland, rose less steeply than those of wheat, barley and rye

[6]Reid, p. 125, stresses the importance of economic hardship as a background to rebellion. Davies, p. 58, shows that harvest failure 'tout court' must be discounted as an explanation of the rebellion as the worst effects were felt six months earlier.

[7]*LP*, IX, 949.

[8]See above, p. 65.

[9]C.S.L. Davies, 'Pilgrimage of Grace Reconsidered', p. 57; W. Hoskins, 'Harvest Fluctuations, 1480-1619', *A.H.R.* 12, pp. 28-46, and J. Thirsk (ed.), *Agrarian History of England and Wales*, vol. IV, p. 19.

between 1534 and 1535, but showed no improvement in the following year. Barley, the main crop in Furness and Cumberland, produced the greatest price rise in 1534-5 and only fell back moderately in the following year. With only the rye crop showing an improvement over the 1534 harvest it seems unlikely that the cumulative effects of two years of dearth could be alleviated by the import of other crops. In the winter of 1536 the Earl of Derby reported a shortage of corn in Lancashire, and in the less self-sufficient Lake Counties conditions are likely to have been much worse.[10]

If the relatively poor harvest and consequent dearth of 1535 was the cause of riots, it can be assumed that the equally bad harvest of 1536 would have caused intense peasant discontent. This being the case, the second precipitating factor, the call to rebel which came from Yorkshire, fell on willing ears.

It seems unlikely that the rebellion in the Lake Counties was planned in advance. Only one incident is recorded which suggests foreknowledge, and that happened in the village of Dent in the West Riding of Yorkshire. Dent and three unknown neighbouring parishes appear to have been sworn to an oath when one William Breyar arrived in mid-September.[11] Breyar reported that rumours were circulating similar to those prevalant in Lincolnshire at the start of the rebellion. Certainly this witness was a rogue, for at some point he had been branded on the hand, and on this occasion he was travelling through the north wearing the King's livery to which he had no right. Possibly it was Breyar himself who was spreading dissent, although he does not appear to have come from other disaffected areas and was not seen in Yorkshire until the rebellion was in progress. Certainly he did not go into the Lake Counties from Dent, and there is no reason to believe that the people there had taken any oath or were planning to rise.

The first official report of any trouble was made by Lord Darcy when, on 6 October, he notified the King of seditions in Dent, Sedbergh, and adjoining parts of the West Riding of Yorkshire.[12] Five days later Sir Thomas Wharton reported the spread of the rising to Kendal, where the inhabitants were 'very troublous'.[13] Probably the stimulus for Kendal to rise came from Dent. Even so these were minor affairs. No doubt harvest failure was taking effect, but the final spark of rebellion was not to arrive for three more days during which time other parts of the region seem to have been quiet.

[10]*LP,* XI, 1066.

[11]*Ibid.,* XI 841.

[12]*Ibid.,*XI, 563.

[13]*Ibid.,* 666.

However, once the impetus was provided, the Lake Counties were as swift to rebel as any other area. This precipitating factor was the call to rise from anonymous correspondents in Yorkshire, and from the leaders of the rebellion in Dent. On 14 October two men from Dent arrived in Kendal. Their stated object was to ask the advice of Sir James Layburn, but there is reason to believe that their intent was to cause Kendal to rise, if not on a voluntary basis then by issuing threats.[14] Having seen Layburn, the two men, George Willen and William Garnet, talked with 'divers light persons of the town', and on the following morning the men of Kendal mustered. An oath was taken to be true to God, King, and to their 'ancient laudable customs'. That done, the two ambassadors returned to Dent.

Kirkby Stephen and Penrith received no such embassies from Yorkshire, but were called to join the rising by letter. Kirkby Stephen may have heard news of the rebellion on 15 October, on which day a minor riot was caused when the curate of the church omitted to call St Luke's as a holiday.[15] On 16 October a letter was received from Richmondshire, and a muster was called at which the vicar of Brough read the following appeal to the assembly.[16]

> Wellbeloved brethren in god we greet you well signifying unto you that we your brethren in Christ have gathered us together and put us in readiness for the maintenance of the faith of god, his laws, and his church, and where abbeys was suppressed we have restored them again and put the religious men into their houses wherefore we exhort you to do the same.

The letter to Penrith does not appear to have been a duplicate, and came from 'beyond Stanesmore'. It asked that the people rise and take an oath to be true

> to god, to the faith of the church, to our sovereign lord the King and to the commonwealth of this realm. And that done that they should restore all the Abeys suppressed . . . and to say such demeanour toward the Scot that no parade of war might ensue but all to be kept in good quiet and peace.

Later, substantial gentlemen were to be sent to join the assembly of commons in Yorkshire. Penrith thus rose separately from Kirkby Stephen, and when the body of the rebels from the Barony of Westmorland arrived to swear the people of Penrith to rebellion the township was already committed.

---

[14]*Ibid.*, XII(1), 914.

[15]*Ibid.*, XII(1), 687(2).

[16]*Ibid.*, PRO, S.P.1, Vol, 117, pp. 46-69. (*LP,* XII(1), 687(1 & 2)).

No evidence exists to show the exact source of the appeals to Kirkby Stephen and Penrith, nor to whom they were particularly directed. That differing oaths were taken by the townships suggests the possibility that where necessary leaders channelled discontent against relevant local issues, as was done by the men of Dent. At Dent and Kendal the defence of ancient custom was added to the manifesto. At Kirkby Stephen, already disturbed by the omission of a holy day, the rebels were content to swear to defend religion alone. At Penrith the leaders were worried about a new war with the Scots and added that issue to their oath.

In each case the impact of the precipitating factor was modified to suit the particular needs of the locality. Once rebellion had successfully been initiated in Kendal, Kirkby Stephen and Penrith, these townships activated rebellion in other areas. However, there can be no doubt that the initial stimulus came from Yorkshire. The demand that the commons should rise and the copy of the rebel oath were accompanied by the words, 'And that they of Westmorland and Cumberland should not fail therof as they of Yorkshire faithfully trusted them. . . . And otherwise doing they must accept and take them as enemies to the christian faith and to the commonwealth.'[17] No such threat was needed to cause the people of the Lake Counties to rise.

The Northern and Southern Movements

The rebellion in the Lake Counties was divided into two separate but associated parts, each centred on the townships in which the messages from Yorkshire had first arrived. In the southern part of the region the most important centre was Kendal, although such places as Dent, Sedbergh, Furness, Cartmel, Lonsdale and southern Westmorland were also involved. In the north the rising centred on Kirkby Stephen, Brough, and neighbouring townships in the Barony of Westmorland, as well as many other communities between Penrith, Carlisle, and Cockermouth. Other isolated townships did at some time join the rebel movements and became associated with one or the other of the main rebel bodies.

Both the southern and northern movements pursued the initial objective of consolidating their area and swearing local gentlemen to the rebel oath. The men of Kirkby Stephen mustered at Sandford Moor whence they moved towards Penrith, attempting on the way to swear local gentlemen such as Sir Thomas Wharton and Sir John Lowther.[18] On reaching Penrith the rebels found it already sworn to

[17]PRO, S.P.1, Vol, 117, pp. 46-69. (*LP*, XII(1), 687(2)).
[18]*LP*, XII(1), 914.

their cause, having independently received the letter from Yorkshire. At Kendal one of the first prominent men to be sworn was a bailiff, William Collins, who became an important rebel leader.[19] However the most influential gentleman of the Kendal area, Sir James Layburn, resisted rebel demands until Friday 27 October. Thus twelve vital days saw little success for the rebels, but for the fact that they were able to consolidate their hold on the immediate area and find strong leaders from their own number. On Saturday 28 October the rebels of the Southern movement mustered at Kellet Moor to prepare for the march on their next objective, Lancaster.

At Penrith events moved rather more swiftly. Finding the town already in arms, the men from the Barony of Westmorland returned home, swearing any townships along their way to the rebel oath.[20] Meanwhile Penrith appointed four leaders under the names 'Charity', 'Faith', 'Poverty' and 'Pity', and by Saturday 21 October swore many surrounding townships to their oath to be true 'to God, the Church, the King, and Commonwealth'.[21] By 23 October, when Caldbeck and Greystoke joined the rebellion, a firm routine for musters was established. Each township elected two representatives to join the leaders, of whom Robert Thompson, the Vicar of Brough, was most prominent under the adopted title 'chaplain of poverty'.

Further musters at Kylwatlinghow and Sandale, on 25 and 27 October respectively, indicated the growing interest of the rebels in Carlisle.[22] A deputation was sent to the city, but when the rebel approaches were rejected an economic boycott was established to cut off communications between Carlisle and the surrounding countryside. Further musters took place at Moota Hill and Broadfield Oak, and on each occasion new deputations were sent to encourage Carlisle to join the rebellion, which it consistently refused to do.

From Kellet Moor the southern movement had advanced on Lancaster, and they met with more success than their allies in Cumberland. The town accepted the rebel oath with little opposition, and thus a strong defensive position was established in the south of the region.[23]

Since the first news of the rebellion had arrived the Earl of Derby had been slowly assembling a force at Lathom.[24] His departure was

[19]*Ibid.*, 914.

[20]*Ibid.*, 687(2).

[21] *Ibid.*,

[22]For the locations of these musters, see map 3, p. 94.

[23]*LP*, XII(1), 914. The rebellion in Lancashire has also been discussed in Haigh, *Lancashire Monasteries*, Chapter Six.

[24]*Ibid.*, XI, 634.

Map 3

TOWNSHIPS INVOLVED IN THE PILGRIMAGE OF GRACE IN THE LAKE COUNTIES 1576-7.

Main Rebel Musters are underlined.

delayed from 10 until 23 October and in all probability he was waiting for the situation to clarify itself.[25] A well-timed incentive in the form of a sizeable commission from the King stirred Derby into action, and by 30 October he had advanced as far as Preston.[26] His initial aim was to march against the force at Whalley which in any case provided the greater threat with its force of three thousand. Even so, he must have been deeply troubled by the presence of the second force at Lancaster. He sent two servants to Lancaster to order the rebels to go home.[27] John Atkinson, the rebel spokesman, naturally declined to disperse his force. He was also unenthusiastic about the suggestion that the loyal and rebel forces should fight out the issue on Bentham Moor. Atkinson seems in fact to have wanted to avoid a major confrontation, and there is little evidence to indicate whether the rebels' plans extended beyond the capture of Lancaster. All he was willing to say was that the rebel body would fight if their Pilgrimage was interrupted.[28]

Both the northern and southern forces were faced for the first time with direct opposition. Yet already they had achieved a considerable amount by raising a large organised movement which was pursuing limited aims within its own region while at the same time supporting the neighbouring Yorkshire rebels.

The Rebels

How many townships and how many individuals joined the rebels is uncertain. Fewer than fifty townships are specifically named as having taken part in the rising, but from the distribution of these it seems that many others were represented in the rebel ranks.[29]

Caution must also be adopted in the assessment of rebel numbers because it is evident that compulsion was used at rebel musters to spur the unwilling. In the first instance the need to swear every town was realised. In the early stages of the rising the men of Dent told prospective rebels at Kendal that their communities had been threatened with spoliation if they would not join the insurrection. When the ringleaders, Brian Jobson and Tom Dockwray, decided to

[25] *Ibid.*, 856.
[26] *LP,* XI, 783.
[27] *Ibid.*, 947(2).
[28] *Ibid.*
[29] See map 3 p. 94.

raise Kendal, they assembled the whole town without harness.[30] Later the commons appear to have joined musters in units of townships, just as they would have done if summoned for the defence of the border. Often they joined with a gentleman or significant leader in the way that Dr Barnard Towneley led the commons of Caldbeck and Sir John Lowther the parishes around Edenhall.

Once the townships were sworn, attention was paid to tardy individuals who had not appeared to take the rebel oath. Robert Pulleyn ordered that the commons should confiscate the goods of any man fleeing the rebel musters.[31] When Parson Roland Threlkeld of Melmerby did not attend a muster, the life of his colleague Barnard Towneley was threatened.[32] Richard Redman of Heysham, who at first refused to take the oath, was taken by two hundred rebels and forced to swear.[33] The rebel leader Robert Thompson, the vicar of Brough, stated that he was originally forced to join the rebel musters.[34] Furness Abbey operated its own recruiting system, inviting tenants to meet one Gilpin, lieutenant to John Atkinson, who was a guest at the abbey.[35] In effect the monks were forcing their tenants to take the rebel oath, and those who were unwilling to do so had no option but to escape.[36] If, as in Lancashire, all men over sixteen years of age were expected to muster, a formidable number must have committed themselves to the rebel oath, many of whom remained to take an active part in the rebellion. Admittedly, there must have been some men who were sworn to the commons' oath against their will, and in the aftermath of rebellion even the most prominent rebels told of threats of violence against their lives, families or goods. If one accepts that this is true in a limited number of cases, the statistics which have survived showing the size of rebel gatherings indicate that involvement was high.

For the Pilgrimage of Grace as a whole Eustace Chapuys estimated in mid-October that 'between thirty and fifty thousand men were in arms'.[37] This estimate is confirmed by a report from Sir Brian Hastings which told of forty thousand rebels.[38] For the Lake

[30]*LP,* XII(1), 914.

[31]*Ibid.,* 687(2).

[32]*Ibid.,* 687(1).

[33]*Ibid.,* 671(2), ii.

[34]*Ibid.,* 687(2).

[35]*Ibid.,* 652.

[36]*Ibid.,* 841(2).

[37]*Ibid.,* XI, 698.

[38]*Ibid.,* 759.

Counties estimates vary enormously. A servant of Lord Darcy, for example, stated that one hundred and forty thousand rebels were up in Lancashire, Cumberland, Westmorland and Durham.[39] A more reasonable figure suggests the presence of fifteen thousand at the Broadfield muster on 30 October.[40] In February 1537 five thousand mustered there again before the attack on Carlisle.[41] To the south, it was reckoned that two thousand men of Dent (which presumably included Sedbergh and other West Riding communities) met five hundred from Kendal at Endmoor.[42] The Earl of Derby estimated that three thousand rebels gathered at Bentham Moor, although he acknowledged that other calculations reached as high as five thousand.[43] Elsewhere, threats were uttered that two thousand men would assemble if Thomas Lamplugh interfered with attacks on tithe barns in Cumberland.[44] At Cockermouth eight hundred men assembled to demand the return of their tithes.[45] In the aftermath of rebellion the Duke of Norfolk wrote that six thousand rebels had given themselves up at Carlisle.[46]

Of these statistics several seem to be well informed. It can safely be concluded that at least three thousand men marched on Lancaster, and that five thousand marched on Carlisle. Including women and children the greatest assembly was that of fifteen thousand at the Broadfield. Twenty thousand men, women and children may have actively supported the rebellion at some stages, and many more may have taken the rebel oath before returning to their homes. If one accepts an estimate for the total population of the region of approximately seventy thousand in 1536, the fact that over one-third of the inhabitants were active rebels indicates a high level of involvement.

It has been established that the rebel force was a large one. More can be discovered about it by looking at the social status or occupation of rebels, details of which have a great bearing on the events of 1536-7.

It is unfortunate that contemporaries failed to see any need to distinguish faces in the crowd according to occupations and social

[39] *Ibid.*, 1086.

[40] *Ibid.*, XII(1), 687(2).

[41] *Ibid.*, 419.

[42] *Ibid.*, 914.

[43] *Ibid.*, XI, 947.

[44] *Ibid.*, XII(1), 18.

[45] *Ibid.*, 319.

[46] *Ibid.*, 498.

status. All too often the participants are referred to as a composite group under the title 'rebels', 'commons', or 'traitors', as this writer has in turn been forced to do.

The occupation of a few individuals can be identified. John Nicholson of Kendal, who brought a bill summoning representatives to Richmond, was described as a woolman.[47] John Dakyn's letters to Kendal were transported by a 'market man'.[48] James Taylor, one of the principals in demanding the bidding of the beads at Kendal, was a shoemaker.[49] William Barret, arrested at Manchester for spreading rumours and being present at the attack on Carlisle, was a tanner from Craven.[50] These occupations indicate an urban element in the commons' ranks, which follows from the fact that the rising appears to have been initiated in the towns. However, even the larger towns were so closely tied to agriculture that one must expect people from agrarian occupations to have been numerically dominant. That this was the case is indicated by the fact that many prominent men in the rebellion were estate officers. William Collins, who led the men of Kendal and represented them at Doncaster, was a bailiff.[51] William Wilkin of Sowerby was the assistant to Robert Jackson, the bailiff there.[52] Christopher Blenkinsop was a bailiff at Stainmore. William Waterman was a reeve at Langton, and Hugh Beale was the bailiff there who in 1534 was entrusted with the care of £66 13s. 4d. which had to be carried to the Countess of Cumberland at Skipton. Finally, Richard Wallour was bailiff at Winton. With the exception of Collins, all these men were hanged in 1537 for their part in the insurrection.[53] Men holding such offices as these are unlikely to have been representative of the whole movement. The fact that they were leaders was probably due to their position as estate officers which gave them considerable advantages not only in status within the peasant ranks but also in such things as literacy. Bailiffs, woolmen (who were working in a prosperous trade in 1536) and freeholders such as the rebel leader Robert Pulleyn were all drawn from the upper and middle ranks of peasant society.

One instance when a classification of rioters was made occurred at

[47]*Ibid.*, 914.

[48]*Ibid.*

[49]*Ibid.*

[50]*Ibid.*, XII(1), 520.

[51]*Ibid.*, 914.

[52]The Library, Chatsworth, Accounts of Reeves and Bailiffs for Westmorland estates of the First Earl of Cumberland, 1534.

[53]See below, pp. 125-6.

Camerton in Cumberland in 1531 and throws light on a useful criterion by which rebels in the Pilgrimage of Grace might be judged.[54] Ninety-five persons were arrested for taking part in a riot against the wife of a local gentleman. Twenty-one of the assailants were described as yeomen, forty-eight as husbandmen, sixteen as labourers, and one as a chaplain. This method of classification was used only once during the Pilgrimage of Grace. The ten men who were hanged at Cartmel were all described as husbandmen. Although only the most tentative statements can be made about the social status of the rebels, in general perhaps the term 'husbandmen' is most appropriate to describe the middling peasantry who were most prominent in the leadership of the rebellion, and possibly, too, in the rank and file. This suggestion is supported by such evidence of the rebels' wealth as has survived.

A list of persons executed in Cumberland and Westmorland in 1537 estimates the value of the goods and chattels forfeited to the King. Of seventy-four men singled out for execution fifty-three originated from twenty Westmorland parishes. Although individual valuations have not survived, the total value of their goods and chattels was put at three hundred marks, an average of £3 15s. 6d. for each man.[55] The estate officers of Sowerby, Stainmore, Langton and

Table 6: Goods and Chattels of executed rebels

Lancelot Richardson of Cockermouth		10s.	9d.
Robert Goodale of Cockermouth	£1	4s.	0d.
John Bewley of Dearham		13s.	0d.
John Wilson of Brigham	£8	12s.	0d.
Percival Hudson of Pardshaw	£1	13s.	10d.
Robert Fisher of Cockermouth		8s.	7d.
Thomas Bell of Cockermouth		1s.	1d.
John Jackson of Embleton	£5	16s.	4d.
Alexander Bank of Wythop	£2	2s.	9d.
John Pearson of Tallentire	£3	18s.	4d.
William Bunting of Greystoke	£6	17s.	8d.
Thomas Burtbeck (?) of Penrith		12s.	11d.
John Stephenson of Penrith	£2	15s.	10d.
William Stephenson of Penrith	£1	14s.	8d.
Richard Cragg of Eaglesfield	£7	4s.	0d.
Christopher Smith of Braithwaite	£2	19s.	2d.
Robert Stephenson of Penrith	£2	6s.	4d.
Sir Edward Penrith of Penrith	£8	0s.	0d.

[54]*LP*, V, 364(ii).

[55]*Ibid*., XII(1), 641.

Winton were included amongst this number. The remaining rebels came from parishes in Cumberland, and details have survived concerning the wealth of eighteen of them.[56] The value of their goods and chattels is indicated in Table 6.

The total value of goods confiscated in Cumberland was £57 11s. 3d., an average of £3 4s. 0d. which compares quite closely with the average for Westmorland. The values of individual possessions varied from £8 12s. 0d. to 1s. 1d. John Wilson, worth the former sum, may have been a substantial landholder if his property matched his personal wealth, while by comparison Thomas Bell was probably a poor man. Of the eighteen values five were of less than one pound and five were of more than four pounds. This may be taken to suggest that, while a full range of peasantry was involved in the rebellion, the middling peasantry predominated. This fact is confirmed by statistics of entry fines paid in 1534 by men who were later to become rebels. The average payment for entry fines on Clifford's Westmorland estates in that year was £1 3s. 2d., while the average payment made by future rebels was £1 3s. 2½d.[57]

It is true that by national standards even the well-to-do peasantry of the Lake Counties were, as the Duke of Norfolk observed, 'poor caitiffs' who reflected the general poverty of this wild and barren region.[58] The average income of the Westmorland rebels was £3 15s. 6d., while the highest income of any of the executed men of Cumberland was £8 12s. 0d. The subsidy rolls for the south of England in the 1520s show that the poorest bailiff was worth twenty marks at Chichester and at High Wycombe forty marks. Most men of bailiff status were worth at least twenty pounds.[59] However, these facts of social status in the south do not disprove that, by the standards of the Lake Counties, many of the rebels were relatively wealthy and certainly were not from the dregs of society. They should therefore not be seen as a poverty-stricken rabble who had nothing to lose by rising against their King. Many were substantial citizens, and they had great influence on the preparation of rebel demands and the execution of rebel plans.

Whether or not the rebels were substantial citizens, law and order in the traditional sense had broken down, and twenty thousand people who were demanding redress of their grievances had to be organised. Otherwise, the region would have collapsed into a state of anarchy which would have served no useful purpose.

[56]PRO, Sheriffs' Accounts, E.199, 7/41.

[57]See above, p. 55.

[58]*LP*, XII(1), 478.

[59]J. Cornwall 'English County Towns in the 1520s', *Ec.H.R.* 2nd ser. 17 (1965).

In fact the rebels were well organised, and it is primarily the evidence of their self-discipline which belies the pejorative labels such as 'the rabble had no leaders' which have since been attached to them.[60] The chief unit of organisation was the muster, regularly experienced by the inhabitants of the region in connection with border raids. After the first spontaneous musters had triggered off a general response to the call to rise, musters were carefully planned in advance and procedure was formalised. The first step was the appointment of leaders. It has been shown that many of the leaders were from the well-to-do peasantry, and certainly their social status and literacy must have recommended them to the mass of rebels. Little is known of many of these men. For example, the four captains of Penrith who adopted the titles Charity, Faith, Poverty and Pity are almost undocumented.[61] Three of them, Anthony Hutton, John Beck and Gilbert Whepdale are mentioned only for their part in the muster of the commons at Caldbeck and in the ceremony at Penrith church. The fourth, Thomas Burtbeck, was the only one to be executed, and his goods were worth 12s. 11d., well below the average.[62] There is also a lack of information about the men responsible for mustering the townships of Kirkby Stephen and Kendal.[63] The only detailed documentation of the leadership of the rebellion relates to the small group of men who dominated at the rebel musters and against whom accusations were made in the aftermath of the Pilgrimage of Grace.

Four laymen may be said to have most influenced the course of the rebellion in the Lake Counties. These were Nicholas Musgrave and Robert Pulleyn of Kirkby Stephen, William Collins the bailiff of Kendal, and John Atkinson who may have come from Dent. Musgrave and Pulleyn were probably freeholders and certainly literate.[64] Collins had dealings in the Duchy Court of Lancaster

---

[60]*Victoria History of England: Cumberland, II,* 50.

[61]*LP,* XII(1) 687(2).

[62]PRO, Sheriffs' Accounts, E.199, 7/41.

[63]Three of the prominent leaders at Kirkby Stephen were Christopher Blenkinsop, Robert Hilton, and Thomas Tebay. Blenkinsop was accused of having forced the vicar of Brough to pray for the Pope, and was executed for his part in the second rebellion. He and Hilton were captains at Sandford Moor. Thomas Tebay is not present in any documentation of the early rebellion, but was on Thomas Clifford's list of wanted men. He hid from Clifford in the steeple at Kirkby Stephen, was prominent in the attack on Carlisle, and was hanged at Mallerstang. At Kendal the leaders were Thomas Dockwray, Brian Jobson, William Garnet and George Willen, who were also captains at Endmoor. Dockwray was a ringleader in threatening the curate at Kendal, and was named by Collins as a prime instigator of rebellion.

[64]Witness their signed letter to Lord Darcy, *LP,* XI, 1080. Pulleyn was a freeholder, for he refused to pay his cornage. *LP,* XII(1), 687(2).

before the rebellion. In 1533 he was accused by the King's deputy butler in Lancashire, Alexander Ratcliff, of shipping forty tons of wine into North Lancashire and refusing to pay the levy which was due. Later he refused to pay for sixty tons at the same place, and for another eighteen tons shipped to Liverpool. Significantly Ratcliff described Collins as having used 'seditious and malicious words and yet doeth like unto a rebellious person'.[65] Nothing is known of John Atkinson's background, but it has been suggested that he may have been a fugitive from Yorkshire, where one Atkinson had attacked a minister in his pulpit for complying with the early devices of the Henrician Reformation.[66]

Several clerics can also be counted amongst the leaders of the rebellion, which belies suggestions that the commons were anti-clerical. Certainly there were threats against priests, but closer scrutiny shows that these threats did not clash with the religious intentions of the rebels. Where priests refused to revert to practices such as beads bidding force was applied to bring compliance. Threats against such priests as Parson Threlkeld of Melmerby undoubtedly arose from commons' displeasure at pluralism and other misuses of clerical offices. Threlkeld was not only rector of Melmerby but also vicar of Lazonby and Dufton, the three offices being valued in 1535 at £12 11s. 4d., £13 1s. 2d. and £19 2s. 6d. respectively.[67] He was the worst example in the region of a wealthy pluralist and absentee cleric of the type that the rebels had determined to overthrow.

On the other hand, those priests who were in unison with the commons were welcomed as leaders, and had an important part to play. The vicars of Sowerby and Edenhall were 'chaplains of poverty' whose duty was to instruct the commons on religion.[68] The vicar of Morland helped to draw up the rebel manifesto for the Lake Counties which was later sent to the conference at Doncaster.[69] William Lancaster, the parson of Beetham, not only prayed for the Pope and bid the beads, but also read rebel communications from Yorkshire to his parishioners, for which he was hanged.[70] The vicar of Dalston was

[65] PRO, D.L.1, Vol.9, R.2. printed in *Pleadings and Depositions in the Duchy Court of Lancaster,* edited by H. Fishwick, L.C.R.S., Vol. XXXV, p. 50.

[66] Dodds, Vol.I, p. 71.

[67] *Valor,* V, pp. 286, 289, 295.

[68] *LP,* XII(1), 687(2), 1259.

[69] *Ibid.,* XI, 1080. See Appendix.

[70] *Ibid.,* XII(1), 914, 1104.

a rebel representative at Carlisle. Sir Edward Penrith, whose office is unknown, was hanged for his part as cross-bearer at rebel musters and marches.[71]

Three clerics played an outstanding role in the leadership of the rebellion. These were Robert Thompson, vicar of Brough, Christopher Howden, vicar of Clapham, and Barnard Towneley, rector of Caldbeck. Thompson was deeply committed to the rising, and was described as 'principal maintainer of the Bishop of Rome'. From the outset when 'the cause of that insurrection was that the vicar of Brough read a letter from Richmondshire' he was always at the centre of events.[72] As 'chaplain of poverty' he proclaimed the four captains of Penrith at every muster, threatened the lives of other clerics, and ordered the boycott of Carlisle. Evidently the rebels regarded Thompson as a prophet and looked to him for guidance.[73]

Christopher Howden, vicar of Clapham, was described by the Earl of Sussex as the steward of the commons, the title by which he was known at the time of the march on Lancaster. He appears to have served the dual function of secretary and spiritual adviser to the rebels. He represented Lord Poverty and was 'the common swearer and counsellor in all that business, and persuaded the people that they should go to heaven if they died in that quarrel'.[74]

Barnard Towneley, rector of Caldbeck and chancellor to the Bishop of Carlisle was also significant within the rising, and indeed was executed thereafter, but his position is an equivocal one. If one accepts the contents of his own confession he would appear to have been an aggrieved cleric, forced into the rebellion against his will, and one against whom a considerable amount of anti-clericalism was directed. When sent to London he was accompanied by the Duke of Norfolk's statement that against him 'I can find nothing since the pardon, nor of no great effect before'.[75] The fact that, despite this, Towneley was excepted from the pardon suggests that his role was perhaps more significant than he would admit. It is likely that his sympathy lay with the rebel cause, for his family were prominent upholders of catholicism in the Burnley area throughout the sixteenth century and indeed since then. Possibly Towneley was forced into the rebellion by a threat against his life. However, thereafter he became a

[71]*Ibid.*, 498, 687.

[72]*Ibid.*, 887(1).

[73]*V.C.H. Cumberland,* II, 51.

[74]*LP,* XII(1), 914.

[75]*Ibid.*, 594.

chaplain of poverty, represented the rebels in negotiations with Carlisle, and was responsible for swearing rebels to the pilgrims' oath.

There can be little doubt that these clerics became deeply involved in the rebellion and exerted a strong influence upon it. They do not appear to have been performing only the limited function of providing the rebels with a rallying cry, for they were an important and committed part of the rebel leadership. Some part in the leadership of the rebellion can also be attributed to the regular clergy.

The three larger monasteries of the Lake Counties were not directly threatened by the suppression of 1536. Even so, they could ignore only with difficulty the assault on their smaller colleagues, or the changes in religious practice which had been made in the past months. Little evidence has survived of the involvement of the priory at Carlisle in the rebellion. This was probably because the priory was contained within the bounds of the only loyal stronghold in Cumberland. In August 1536 there had been a riot there, allegedly at the command of Bishop Kyte of Carlisle.[76] The priory may have been involved, but evidence is lacking. During the rebellion at least two canons, Richard Huttwythe and William Florens, were amongst the rebels.[77] They negotiated with the town on behalf of the rebels before the truce was announced. It is also possible that the Prior, Christopher Slee, was deposed from his office as a consequence of the rebellion, for between 1536 and 1537 he was replaced by Lancelot Salkeld, a place-man who finally surrendered the priory and became the first Dean of Carlisle.[78]

Documentation for the part played in the rebellion by the Abbey of Holm Cultram is somewhat better. Abbot Carter appears to have firmly supported the cause of the Pilgrims, but was unwilling to commit his own person to rebellion. In the early stages of rebellion the abbot ordered his brethren and tenants to attend the muster at Kylwatlinghow.[79] Only later was he persuaded to go himself by the vicar of Brough.[80] As a man of considerable status, he was naturally appointed as a commissioner to negotiate with the city of Carlisle. On the first occasion when he went to the city on the rebels' behalf he was met with a rebuff. He was unwilling to go at all on the second occasion, but despite this he was concerned to give forty shillings to the rebels at

[76]*Ibid.*, XI, 319.
[77]*Ibid.*, XIII(1), 687(1).
[78]Bouch and Jones, p. 55.
[79]*LP,* XII(1), 1259.
[80]*Ibid.*, XII(1), 687(1).

Penrith in order that representatives could be sent into Yorkshire.[81] Moreover, this enthusiasm did not abate during the later part of the rebellion, for he was delighted to hear of the new muster at Broadfield Oak in mid-February 1537. With the words 'All Mighty God prosper them, for if they speed not the Abbey is lost',[82] he summoned his brethren and tenants and commanded them to join the rebels. In the event the host gathered in Holm Cultram church, and the abbot commanded his deputy steward, Cuthbert Musgrave, to lead them to join the rebel muster. Musgrave refused, and as the abbot would not lead the tenants himself, the company dispersed.[83]

Like Abbot Carter, the Abbot of Furness was concerned above all with self preservation, but the monks there also expressed a more general dissatisfaction with the policies of King Henry VIII. Possibly the concern of the brethren with the dissolution, which was not as yet a threat to Furness, was stimulated by the presence of four monks from Sawley abbey, which had been suppressed earlier in the year.[84] The abbot was sympathetic to their predicament and encouraged them to return into Yorkshire when news of the rebellion there came to Furness. Pyle then decided on the course which the abbey should take to maximise its chances of survival. Simply, this course was to make sure that the abbey was represented on both sides. Before the rebels arrived at Furness, the abbot fled to the Earl of Derby, instructing the brethren of the abbey 'to do the best they can do to the commons and he will do the best he can with the King'.[85] Most of the monks were happy to throw in their lot with the commons, and by 31 October the abbey was firmly identified with the Pilgrimage of Grace. Gilpin, a lieutenant to the rebel leader Atkinson, was welcomed at Furness, and the monks appear to have recruited their tenants for him.[86] The Prior, Brian Gardner, instructed some tenants to attend Gilpin at the monastery on pain of death and of pulling down their houses.[87] Once assembled, the tenants were led to Dalton, and the men of Dalton, Stainton and Walney were commanded to join them with arms and armour. All tenants were advised by the monks to 'agree with them as we have done' for 'now must they stick together or else never, for if they sit down both you and the Holy Church is undone, and if they

[81]*Ibid.*, 687(2) and 1259.
[82]*Ibid.*, 1259.
[83]*Ibid.*, 1259(4).
[84]*Ibid.*, 841(4).
[85]*Ibid.*, 849.
[86]*Ibid.*, 652, 841(3).
[87]*Ibid.*, 841(2).

lack company we will go with them and live and die with them to defend their Godly pilgrimage'.[88] Some money, either £20 or £23 6s. 8d., was given to the rebels to help them, and several of the monks, including Michael Hammerton, the cellarer, joined the rebels.

It would be wrong to say that any of these commons and clerics alone dominated the leadership of the rebellion in the Lake Counties. In fact, one reason why no single person achieved greater prominence was that the process of selecting leaders was essentially democratic. At the larger musters, such as those at Moota Hill, Cartlogan Thorns and Broadfield Oak, any communities which joined the rebels elected two representatives to join the leadership.[89] In other words, rebel government appears to have been by committee. At the head of the committee was a figure of considerable status, taking upon himself the name of 'Captain of Poverty' and backed by a clerical secretary. However, the anonymity of the Captain of Poverty in the north of the region and 'Lord Poverty' in the south suggests that their power was only nominal, and that these men may have been only figureheads. Even Robert Thompson, a man to whom has been attributed considerable power in the rebel ranks, said in his own confession that he was forced to do 'the best that I could and as they commanded for they were more than twenty captayns both wilful and unruly'.[90]

The same procedure appears to have been followed at most musters. Firstly, newcomers were given the rebel oath 'to be true to god almighty and the faith of our holy mother the church to our sovereign lord the King and commonwealth'.[91] Then the crier made the proclamation of rebel aims, and gave instructions to the rank and file. Thereafter the priests moved amongst the rebels instructing them in the faith, and the captains discussed future plans.[92] This done, the location of the next muster was announced and the whole body moved on.

The men who attended musters appear to have done so at their own charge. Thompson testified that 'all the time that I was amongst them I knew no man that had others horse or harness; in body or goods: other than made any cost but of himself'.[93] One of the primary rebel instructions was that the commons should 'keep charity and peace, and that no man steal nor rob, nor reeve, nor meet with other

[88]*Ibid.*, 841(3).

[89]*Ibid.*, 687(2), from original in PRO, S.P.1, 117, pp. 46-69.

[90]PRO, Exchr. T.R. Misc. Books, 119, pp. 159-69, (*LP,* XII(1), 687(4)).

[91]PRO, S.P.1, 117, pp. 46-69, *LP,* XII(1), 687(2).

[92]*LP,* XII(1), 687(2).

[93]PRO, E.36, Vol. 119, pp. 159-69, (*LP,* XII(1), 687(2)).

mans goods on pain of death'.[94] In general this instruction was followed. The confiscation of gentlemen's goods and the breaking open of tithe barns was official policy. They were not random mob raids, but organised attacks with a purpose in mind. Gentlemen's goods were taken in order to force them to join the rebels, and tithe corn was shared out to alleviate the shortage.[95] Rebel income did not derive from thefts. The monks of Furness gave them over £20, and the Abbot of Holm Cultram gave them 20s., and other contributions may have been made by rebel sympathisers to cover the costs of representatives going to the meeting at York.[96] Elsewhere the rebels appear to have collected small sums from amongst themselves which amounted to a communal levy.[97] The rapid movement of the musters ensured that no single area would have to bear the burden of feeding the rebels for too long. How the process of maintaining the force was organised is unknown. However, for those men who were involved in the leadership of the rebellion, hospitality appears to have been provided. William Collins, for example, entertained Atkinson while he was staying at Kendal.[98]

For an unrestrained and angry crowd the rebels of the Lake Counties appear to have acted with great common sense. They were, after all, on their own home ground, and the ideals which they were seeking to defend precluded any great extremism. It would be surprising if there had been no robberies, threats of violence, or vendettas, for these are an inevitable part of any insurrection. However, remembering the general lawlessness of the region which was manifest even in years of peace, the rebels were well ordered. Threats against the lives of clerics and unpopular gentlemen were not carried out, and apart from the pursuit of explicit rebel grievances the only personal animus arose against such men as the unpopular Peter Middleton. Moreover, before the attack on Kirkby Stephen by Thomas Clifford in 1537, there is no evidence that any people were killed in the region as a consequence of the rebellion.

Relations with the Gentry

In consolidating their strength the rebels had to deal with their first and most immediate opposition, the lords and gentlemen of the region.

[94]PRO, E.36, Vol. 119, p. 159, (*LP,* XII(1), 687(4)).

[95]*Ibid.*, XII(1), 18.

[96]*Ibid.*, 841(3), ii, and 1259.

[97]For one example of this at Beetham, See below, p. 120.

[98]*LP,* XII(1), 959.

Whereas in mid-Lancashire and the Sawley area of Yorkshire the rebels were taking and swearing gentlemen as their future leaders, in the Lake Counties the gentlemen were seen as a threat to the rebellion. The rebels, at their most outspoken, would have 'no gentlemen to be their captains', and few gentlemen moved freely in their ranks.[99]

Several gentlemen appear to have been singled out by the rebels as potential threats to the rising. It has been mentioned that at Kendal they were determined to take Sir James Layburn before marching against Lancaster and leaving their homes undefended behind them.[100] On Saturday 14 October, when news of the insurrection in Yorkshire first reached Kendal, Sir James ordered the townspeople not to meddle.[101] On the following day a muster took place at Tarney Banks, and although Sir James left his seal with the rebels he refused to take the rebel oath. Eight days later he was still holding aloof, and for the first time the rebels decided to use force against this much-respected figure. On Tuesday 24 October the rebels departed for Layburn's house, but they were forced to turn back because of bad weather. On Wednesday they partially spoiled his house, but acted with restraint after receiving a promise that he would now join them. Spoliation was further postponed on Thursday when Nicholas Layburn, brother of Sir James, gave the rebels £20, and on Friday 27 October, thirteen days after the original appeal to him, Sir James was sworn and followed the rebels to Lancaster.[102] The case of Layburn demonstrates the tenacity with which the rebels attempted to bring in a particular gentleman, and much time was wasted because the rebels were at first unwilling to use force. In all probability this was because Layburn was a popular figure who in past years had successfully foiled Clifford attempts to dominate Kendal.

The rebel attitude towards less popular gentlemen was less restrained. The first priority of the men of Kirkby Stephen was to take Sir Thomas Wharton.[103] By the time that they reached his house on 16 October Wharton had escaped. He was not at any time taken by the rebels, despite the production of bills demanding his capture.[104] However, the rebels' activity had the desired effect of neutralising Wharton, for he remained in hiding throughout the rising and was unable to organize any effective opposition.

[99] PRO, S.P.1, 117, pp. 146-69. (*LP,* XII(1), 1034, and *LP,* XII(1), 687(2)).

[100] For the importance of Sir James to Kendal, see above, pp.38-9.

[101] *LP,* XII(1), 914.

[102] *Ibid.,* 914.

[103] *Ibid.,* 687(2).

[104] *Ibid.,* XI, 1046.

Another gentleman high on the rebels' list of potential enemies was the sheriff of Cumberland, Sir Thomas Curwen.[105] He was active in the royal service in the Lake Counties throughout October and November without being captured or sworn. Only in January, when tithe barns were raided and a new attack on Carlisle was threatened did Curwen flee to Sheriff Hutton, fearing that the rebels were intent on his death.[106] He reported that throughout the rising in the Lake Counties the rebels were watching for him, and certainly when a messenger was taken who was thought to have been carrying Curwen's and Wharton's letters only the demand for a fair trial saved the man from execution. Of all the gentlemen in the region, Curwen appears to have been most diligent in serving the King. He said to Norfolk that he would rather suffer death than be untrue to the King, and Norfolk described him as 'the man of all other that may best serve in Cumberland'.[107]

Highest on the rebels' list of enemies were the Cliffords. On one occasion when Henry Lord Clifford, the Earl of Cumberland's son, left Carlisle he was intercepted by a group of rebels, but he turned and rode away provoking cries that he would not escape so easily next time.[108] At one stage the King was informed of the capture of Lord Clifford, but this seems to have been unsubstantiated. Lord Darcy wrote 'I do not know that Lord Clifford is taken',[109] and indeed once he had reached the safety of Carlisle he appears to have spent most of his time there before riding on to London in January.[110]

If, with the exception of Layburn, the rebels failed to take these prominent men, they nevertheless achieved their ambition of neutralising the opposition. With their enemies in hiding, or besieged within the walls of Carlisle, the security of the region was temporarily ensured.

The capture of gentlemen was not simply an attempt to neutralise potential opposition to the rising. The adherence of gentlemen to the rebels' demands could also provide immediate redress of some grievances. To this effect the men of Kendal proclaimed that 'every man take his land's lord and ye shall have need, as we did in Kendal land, then shall ye speed'.[111] Primarily the rebels saw in the

[105]Curwen was made Sheriff in December 1536. *LP*, XI, 1217(23).

[106]*LP*, XII(1), 185.

[107]*Ibid.*, XII(2), 248, PRO, S.P.1, Vol. 122, p. 237, (*LP*, XII(2), 248).

[108]*Ibid.*, XII(1), 7.

[109]*LP*, XI, 1096.

[110]*Ibid.*, XII(1), 71.

[111]*Ibid.*, XI, 892(3).

taking of gentlemen an opportunity to stop the enhancement of gressums or entry fines, and this may have been as important to them as the taking of the oath itself. This can be seen in the prolonged negotiations with Sir James Layburn. The rebels were not satisfied with his initial statement concerning gressums that 'he would do as other men did'.[112] Later a guarantee concerning customs was obtained from parson Nicholas Layburn, who put his brother's seal to the commons' book.[113] Walter Strickland, a young gentleman of Sizergh followed suit, and, if all the gentlemen who took the rebel oath at Kendal were forced to do the same, Sir Robert Bellingham, William Lancaster and Richard Ducket must also have acceded to rebel custom.

In the Barony of Westmorland gressums were again high on the rebels' list of priorities, and it may be assumed that Sir John Lowther, Sir William and Sir Edward Musgrave, John Warcop and John Legh were compelled to 'seal to their demands touching ingressions'.[114] Sir William Musgrave, the man responsible for the Dacre trial of 1534, was able to move freely from Carlisle to Skipton.[115] One explanation for the ability of this most unpopular figure to cross rebel territory unmolested is that he had given way to the commons on what was to them the fundamental issue of gressums.

If the rebels succeeded with Musgrave and others, they failed with their intention to take Peter Middleton of Castlerigg, Keswick, who was one of the most notorious landlords of the region. Middleton's estates had been regularly in contention since they were granted to him in 1531.[116] As well as being unpopular with the Ratcliffe family, whose estates Middleton leased, he also had alienated the tenantry.[117] Amongst the charges laid against him by Dame Alice Ratcliffe were that he had allowed the land to go to waste, killed the deer in the park, and disturbed the tenants of Castlerigg and Talentire.[118] Middleton managed to evade the charges with the help of influential friends such as Sir Thomas Wharton. However, during the Pilgrimage of Grace he became exposed to his tenants' desire for vengeance. In a case in the court of Chancery in 1537 he testified that

[112]*Ibid.*, XII(1), 914.

[113]*Ibid.*

[114]*Ibid.*, XII(1), 687(2).

[115]*Ibid.*, XI, 1242.

[116]PRO, STAC.2, 17/204, 26/219, 26/319, 27/417.

[117]PRO, C.1, 727/12, 853/43, 878/6-7.

[118]PRO, C.1, 878/6-7.

in this great insurrection and traitorous rebellion . . . most of the tenants and inhabitants dwelling on this manor . . . did traitorously assemble themselves together and would have enforced your orator to take their part. However, your orator was glad to in forcible manner to assemble his friends to keep and defend his house lying within an isle.[119]

The siege of the small island on Derwentwater, still marked on ordnance survey maps as the site of a manor house, lasted for fifteen weeks, from October 1536 to January 1537. Middleton did not feel safe until the arrival of the Duke of Norfolk in the region in mid-February. During those weeks the threshers were put out of his tithe barns, and when Thomas Lamplugh attempted to intervene on Middleton's part he was threatened with the prospect of a force of two thousand men rising against him.[120] Meanwhile, the distribution of grain from tithe barns fed the rebels and alleviated the frustrations which they must have felt at not being able to pin Middleton down to fixed customs. It is even possible that it was on the island that Sir Thomas Wharton was hiding, and his capture would have been a great prize.

With John Legh, as with Peter Middleton, the desire to enforce an adherence to traditional custom was mixed with a desire for revenge. Legh was a notorious encloser of land in Cumberland in the years preceding the Pilgrimage of Grace, and he was also a man willing to buy the King's favour by enforcing more stringent economic charges on royal estates.[121] Legh was captured by the rebels, forced to attend musters, and no doubt added his seal to an economic agreement with the commons. However, it is unlikely that he willingly joined the rebel ranks, something of which he was later accused by Sir Thomas Wharton.[122] The rebellion provided the local peasantry with the opportunity to get their own back for long standing grievances against Legh, and that gentleman's attendance at musters was clearly a result of fear rather than sympathy.

However, revenge was less important to the rebels than the settlement of economic issues. The only clear case of revenge being pursued under the cover of rebellion did not involve the peasantry at

[119]*Ibid.*, 859/50.

[120]*LP,* XII(1), 18.

[121]See above, pp. 69-70.

[122]*LP,* XII(1), 904.

all, but was a family feud amongst the gentry.[123] The rebels, having settled as many of their problems as possible within the region by capturing gentlemen and securing agreements concerning traditional custom, now had to look elsewhere. It was important that these temporary successes which had been achieved by confrontation with lords and gentlemen should now be legitimised by King and Parliament. To achieve this end and to obtain satisfaction on broader issues of complaint it was necesssary to make and maintain firm connections with the main body of the Pilgrimage in Yorkshire.

The Lake Counties and the Yorkshire Pilgrimage

There had been little contact with Yorkshire since the arrival of the letters announcing the outbreak of rebellion. The decision which faced the rebel musters at Carlisle and Lancaster was both crucial and dangerous, for the rebellion so far had been limited in nature. The confrontation which both movements now faced required a commitment to fight the King's representatives, something which would add a new dimension to the rising.

However, events had moved swiftly in Yorkshire and such a confrontation had already been resolved there, at least in the short term. At York Robert Aske had stamped his own impression on the rebellion by presenting the 'Oath of Honourable Men'.

> Ye shall not enter into this our Pilgrimage of Grace for the Commonwealth but only for the love that ye do bear unto Almighty God his faith, and to the Holy Church militant and the maintenance thereof, to the preservation of the King's person and his issue, to the purifying of the nobility, and to expulse all villein blood and evil councillors against the Commonwealth from his Grace and his Privy Council of the same. And that ye shall not enter into our said Pilgrimage for no particular profit to yourself, not to do any displeasure to any private person, but by counsel of the Commonwealth, nor slay nor murder for no envy, but in your hearts put away fear and dread, and take afore you

[123]On the death of Lancelot Highmore of Bewaldwath his estates descended to his wife Agnes, but this was fought against by Lancelot's brother Anthony, who claimed that the estates should descend through the male line. In 1533 servants of Anthony Highmore attacked Dame Agnes's tenants and stole some property, as well as damaging the manor house by pulling off the thatch and pouring '30 or 40 galons of water opon ther hede that were withyn the same'. Anthony continued his activities in 1535 and 1536, but was at each stage thwarted by the courts. In January 1537 it was reported that 'was the holde wyffe put forthe of hyr posession by hymar that make tytyll to the lande', although whether Dame Agnes was able to gain redress is unknown. PRO, STAC.2, 23/292; C.1, 824/16; STAC.2, 32/145; and *LP,* XII(1), 185 from original in PRO, S.P.1, Vol. 114, pp. 259-60.

the Cross of Christ, and in your hearts His faith, the Restitution of the Church, the suppression of these heretics and their opinions, by all the holy contents of this book.[124]

The next rebel target was Pontefract Castle. With the exception of Pontefract, Newcastle, Scarborough and Skipton all towns east of the Pennines were in the Pilgrims' hands. The town of Pontefract also favoured the rebels, but the castle was closed against them. Moreover, within the castle was assembled a gathering of about forty lords, knights, gentlemen and clerics of Yorkshire of whom the most notable were Lord Darcy, Sir Robert Constable, and the Archbishop of York. On 19 October Aske gained permission to address them, and stressed not only the spiritual poverty of the north, but also the decline of the northern economy which had been exacerbated by recent events such as the closure of monasteries. His oratory won most of the assembled company to his side, and on 21 October Lord Darcy surrendered Pontefract castle. He used the pretext that the lives of his grandchildren were in jeopardy if he refused the rebel demands, but subsequent events show that he was only providing himself with some justification should the course of the rebellion turn against him. Thereafter his commitment to the Pilgrimage was total, as was that of Sir Robert Constable. Only the Archbishop of York remained consistently opposed to the rising, and he preached against it at a Pilgrims' service.

In winning over these gentlemen Aske had achieved a major victory. The next challenge was to come from the Duke of Norfolk, the Earl of Shrewsbury and the King's army which had marched to Doncaster. In the event of a battle taking place, the balance of power favoured the rebels. England north of the Don was almost entirely under their control. They had a well disciplined army of about 30,000, whereas Norfolk's 8,000 men were hastily assembled and lacking in confidence. Norfolk was well aware of the insecurity of his position, and wanted to negotiate with the rebels rather than fight them. He therefore requested that four representatives meet him at Doncaster to discuss their grievances. Many of the rebels wanted to exploit their superiority to the full, and inflict a major defeat on the King's army. Others remembered Norfolk as the victor at Flodden Field, and trusted him enough to risk negotiation. They were also well aware of the contradiction between their oath of loyalty to the King and implications of defeating his army in battle. The defeat of Norfolk's army would take the rebellion into a new phase tantamount to civil war. Many rebels therefore saw negotiation as the route to success

---

[124]*LP*, XI, printed in Fletcher, *Tudor Rebellions*, p. 122.

while the rebels were able to talk from a position of strength. Aske led the majority into an acceptance of Norfolk's proposals and on 27 October, while the rebel army drew up outside Doncaster, their representatives presented a petition which summed up the general aims of the rising.[125] If at this moment Norfolk attempted to win over the rebel leaders by subterfuge, he failed. The petition was accepted and it was agreed that it should be taken to the King by two gentlemen from the rebel ranks, Sir Ralph Ellerker and Robert Bowes. Until a reply was received both sides agreed to observe a truce, and messages were sent to other areas of rebellion by both sides to preclude the possibility of any incident promoting the renewal of hostility.

The confrontations at Lancaster and Carlisle were ended by the arrival of news of the truce. On 30 October a muster took place at Broadfield Oak near Carlisle, but a deputation from the city produced a copy of the proclamation announcing the truce.[126] At first the Cumberland rebels were suspicious of the document, and they sent messengers to Penrith to clarify the situation. A new muster took place at Broadfield Oak on 3 November, and on this occasion in the absence of Robert Thompson the rebels were persuaded by Sir Christopher Dacre to accept the proclamation and disperse. They went home with the assurance that henceforth they would be admitted into Carlisle without recrimination.[127]

The arrival of Berwick, the herald-at-arms, resolved the impasse at Preston. He brought orders that the Earl of Derby should disperse his company.[128] The rebels at Lancaster received similar word from Aske, and they too dispersed to await further news from London and Yorkshire.

There can, however, be little doubt that the leaders of the rebellion in Yorkshire were ignorant of the course of events in the Lake Counties, for the representatives nominated for the region were strangely chosen, including many men who were at odds with the rebels, or reluctant neutrals.[129] The role of most of the gentlemen

[125]This petition was later to be amplified into the full statement of rebel demands, the Pontefract Articles.

[126]*LP,* XII(1), 687(2).

[127]*Ibid.,* 687(1).

[128]*Ibid.,* XI, 900, 901.

[129]*LP,* XI, 1155. The representatives for the Lake Counties were: Westmorland; Sir John or Lancelot Lowther, Sir Thomas Wharton, Sir William Musgrave, William Lancaster and eight others. Cumberland; Sir Thomas Curwen, Sir John Lamplugh, John Legh, two other gentlemen and eight commons. Kendal and Lonsdale; Richard Duckett, William Kynvett, Sir Robert Bellingham, Walter Strickland and six commons. Furness; Richard Kirkby, Mr. Bardesay, Gervase Middleham, Richard Newman and six others. Cartmel; Nicholas Thornborough and three yeomen.

summoned as rebel representatives has already been examined. Sir Thomas Wharton, Sir William Musgrave, and Sir Thomas Curwen were positively hostile to the rebellion. John Legh, William Lancaster, Sir John Lamplugh and Sir Robert Bellingham played equivocal roles but were at most passive towards the rebels, and in the end helped to bring about their destruction. Lamplugh was responsible for the arrest of Sir Francis Bigod in February 1537 but did little else.[130] Sir John Lowther, the remaining gentleman of importance, rode freely among the rebels and was sworn to their oath, but this was only to enable him to carry out his duties as deputy warden of the march, a function which was advantageous to rebels and loyalists alike.[131] Lowther was nominated by the rebels as a representative to negotiate on their behalf at Carlisle, but did not reciprocate the faith of the rebels in him.

Of all the gentlemen nominated only two appear to have gone to Pontefract, these being Sir Walter Strickland and Richard Duckett.[132] Both were sworn to the rebel oath on the first day of the insurrection at Kendal, had agreed to abide by traditional custom, and had been taken to Kellet Moor and Lancaster, although they played no significant part there. During the early months of 1537 Duckett was prominent in attempting to maintain the peace at Kendal by urging the rebels not to rise again, and he was later said to have arrested John Atkinson, the rebel leader.[133] On the assumption that neither Strickland nor Duckett were prominent at the conference at York, the representation for the Lake Counties remained entirely in the hands of the commons.

The letter which summoned the representatives of Kendal to York, and informed them of the first meeting at Doncaster required the rebels in the Lake Counties 'to send of every parish one gentleman and two yeomen, of the tallest and wisest men, well horsed and harnessed, to Pontefract that of them might be taken out a certain to meet with the Duke of Norfolk at the next meeting at Doncaster'.[134] In response Kendal sent William Collins, bailiff of Kendal, who was to be their most prominent delegate, with Edward Manser, Anthony Langhorne, John Eyrey and Harry Batemen, Strickland and Duckett.[135] Kirkby Stephen received the summons from Robert Pulleyn, the only

[130]*LP,* XII(1), 401.

[131]*Ibid.,* 687(2).

[132]*Ibid.,* 914.

[133]*Ibid.,* 825.

[134]*Ibid.,* XI, 1155.

[135]*Ibid.,* XII(1), 914.

representative of the Lake Counties known to have attended the first meeting with Norfolk in response to an earlier summons from Robert Aske.[136] Pulleyn had brought back a copy of the grievances which had been dispatched to London with Ellerker and Bowes, and when more detailed complaint was demanded he organised a committee of twenty-four persons to devise suitable articles of complaint for consideration at Pontefract. With Nicholas Musgrave, the second signatory to the completed document, and other unnamed captains, Pulleyn then returned into Yorkshire.

The achievements of these representatives at Pontefract and Doncaster were significant. William Collins was particularly concerned to help the priories of Cartmel and Conishead who had written to Kendal requesting help without which 'all they have shall be taken from them'.[137] The canons of Conishead were restored to their house sometime before 16 October, after which time they do not appear to have played any great part in the rebellion. In fact, the government seems to have been ignorant of the fact that the monks were restored until examinations were made after the rebellion.[138] The canons of Cartmel were restored sometime before 30 October. With the exception of the prior who fled to the Earl of Derby they seem to have supported the rising. In answer to letters from the two houses Collins took their case to John Dakyn, Vicar General of the diocese of Richmond. He was persuaded to write to the Priors ordering them to re-enter the suppressed houses.[139] Although they were already back in, the letter from Dakyn added some legitimacy to their situation. Musgrave and Pulleyn, carrying their complaints which were specifically addressed to Lord Darcy, exhibited them to Aske who 'allowed the most part of them'.[140] Articles concerning enclosures and entry fines subsequently appeared amongst the twenty-four demands presented to the Duke of Norfolk. It was also established, at least in the mind of Pulleyn, that rosaries could now be bid in the old way, and confirmation was to come from the convocation of northern clergymen which was appointed by the rebel leaders to meet at the last Doncaster conference.

Letters were dispatched to the clergy of the Lake Counties asking for their opinions on certain issues, but were returned unanswered by timid clerics who 'referred their minds to the archbishop of York with

[136]*Ibid*., XII(1), 687(2).

[137]*Ibid*., XII(1), 914.

[138]*Ibid*., XII(1), 787, 914.

[139]*Ibid*., XI, 1279.

[140]PRO, E.36, Vol. 119, p. 162, (*LP*, XII(1), 687(4)).

such learned counsel as they heard say would be at Pontefract'.[141] Pulleyn, who intercepted this letter, appears to have been angry that no more positive reply was offered.

Despite this setback, the representatives of the Lake Counties were able to return home after successfully airing their grievances. The regular clergy were now authorised to return to their priories, and religious ceremonies could be carried out by the secular clergy in the traditional fashion. Economic grievances had been incorporated into a document of complaint which had the full support of the Pilgrims of Grace behind it. The participation of the rebels of the Lake Counties in the negotiations in Yorkshire is significant because it shows that they did not look upon their rising as separate from the Pilgrimage of Grace as a whole. As one section of a larger movement they took part in a rebellion which shared many of their grievances, and often their enthusiasm exceeded that of their neighbours. This being the case, the rising in the Lake Counties should not be seen as an isolated movement, but rather as one part of a larger movement, at least as far as the communication difficulties of the time would allow.

Uneasy Truce

While the rebels' manifesto was being compiled the terms of the truce were not entirely observed by the inhabitants of the Lake Counties. In both the north and south of the region the frenzied activity of October gave way to small-scale disorder in November. The Furness area had been deeply involved in the rebellion since the day of the march against Lancaster, at which time a large muster had taken place at Hawkshead.[142] The Abbot of Furness, who had fled to the Earl of Derby, at the same time ordered his brethren to help the rebels, thus ensuring that the abbey was represented on both sides. Other stirrings took place in Dent, Sedbergh and north Lancashire possibly at the express command of Robert Aske.[143] The Earl of Derby, worried by this activity, ordered his servants and friends to be ready to pursue the rebels and harry them from the rear should they march towards Lancaster again.[144] This order in itself promoted new musters by the commons, and it seemed likely that a confrontation might after all take place. Hurried correspondence between the Earl of Shrewsbury on one side and Lord Darcy on the other confirmed that a breach of the

[141]*LP,* XII(1), 687(4), from original in PRO, E.36, Vol. 119, p. 162.

[142]*Ibid.,* XI, 892.

[143]*Ibid.,* 995, 1009, 1046.

[144]*Ibid.,* 1092.

truce was in the interest of neither, and the Earl of Derby was ordered to hold his men at the ready but not to assemble them until commanded to do so.[145]

Other disturbances took place in Cumberland. On 6 November the Earl of Cumberland reported that the commons of the northern counties were 'wilfully set and minded . . . rather for war than for peace'.[146] Somerset herald told Lord Darcy in mid-November that a vast number of people were still in arms in Cumberland, Westmorland and the Bishopric of Durham, and he was probably ignorant of the fact that on 15 November Richard Dacre led a new muster at Caldbeck.[147]

During November the loyal and rebel sides had become increasingly suspicious of one another. This was largely because of the prolonged absence of Ellerker and Bowes. The situation in the Lake Counties in December remained unsettled. Early in the month Lord Monteagle wrote that 'the rebels are about Kendal as cruelly minded as ever'.[148] To the north, despite Sir William Musgrave's comment that 'Cumberland and Westmorland are not so ill disposed as was first thought', rebel activities continued, but were only one cause of the disturbances.[149] Whereas the King's representatives in Yorkshire were trying to unite the rival families of Clifford and Dacre to restore peace, in fact their feud was continuing.[150] On 9 December Richard Dacre on one side and Henry Lord Clifford and Sir William Musgrave on the other openly clashed within the walls of Carlisle.[151] Law and order was thus not re-established, and in mid-December these 'high and wild' counties were still 'far out of frame'.[152]

On 19 December the pardon was proclaimed at Kendal, but the uneasy situation there did not improve.[153] The most likely reason for the continued lawlessness is that, like many of the rebels in Yorkshire, the men of Kendal were dissatisfied with the terms of the truce and the delay in royal action. On New Year's Day William Collins, the bailiff at Kendal, attempted to calm the commons by reading the King's pardon in the church.[154] Only the intervention of the parson,

[145]*Ibid.*, 1134.
[146]*Ibid.*, 993.
[147]*Ibid.*, 1086, 1331.
[148]*Ibid.*, 1232.
[149]*Ibid.*, 1228.
[150]*Ibid.*, 1207.
[151]*Ibid.*, 1331.
[152]*Ibid.*, 1294.
[153]*Ibid.*, 1392.
[154]*Ibid.*, XII(1), 7.

Nicholas Layburn, saved the bailiff from threatened death at the hands of the congregation. Elsewhere men were still being sworn to the 'custom of Kendal', and rebel activity was reported at Heysham.[155]

There was trouble, too, at Cartmel. This resulted from the conflict between the restored canons and the farmers to whom the priory lands had been granted away. The farmers complained that the canons were taking away corn which no longer belonged to them.[156] Clarencieux herald commanded that the farmers should not be disturbed in the possession of their lands or tithes. In response to this the monks pleaded that they had been left with no resources. The rebel leaders attempted to make a compromise by confirming the proclamation of Clarencieux 'except ye will of your charity help the brethren there somewhat toward their board, till my Lord of Norfolk come again and take further order therein'.[157] This attempt at a settlement proved to be inadequate, and the situation degenerated until mid-February when the King's farmer, one Thomas Holcroft, tried to take away the priory's corn.[158] The canons and some tenants opposed him, for which they were arraigned on a charge of treason.

On 3 January tithe barns in Cumberland were broken open, and new musters were held.[159] The Earl of Cumberland thought that a new rising was imminent, and on 21 January Sir Thomas Curwen reported stirrings in Cumberland when he said that from 'Plomlande to Mongcastor ys all on slowghter'.[160] Being in fear for his life, Curwen fled the area this time.

On Saturday 3 February new interest was stimulated in the problem of tithes by the arrival of letters from Richmond summoning representatives to attend a council on the following Monday.[161] According to William Collins the letter was delivered to his maid, and when she brought it to him she reported that it had been delivered by John Nicholson, a woolman. Nicholson was searched for, and when he declared that the letter had come from Nicholas Musgrave, Parson Layburn declared that 'he was worthy to sit by the heels therefore in the dungeon, and cast him the bill again and bade him deliver it again where he had it'.[162] The implication of Collins's confession is that he

[155]*Ibid.*, 671.

[156]*Ibid.*, 914.

[157]*Ibid.*

[158]*Ibid.*

[159]*LP,* XII(1), 18.

[160]PRO, S.P.I., 114, pp. 259-60, (*LP,* XII(1), 185).

[161]*Ibid.*, XII(1), 671.

[162]*Ibid.*, 914.

agreed with Layburn, but in fact he called the men of Kendal to the loft at the court. He showed the assembled company the letters, and men were chosen to go to Richmond.[163] The message was relayed to other parishes, including Windermere where the letter was destroyed.[164] Finally John Savell, Leonard Hugyn and John Nelson left for Richmond as Kendal representatives, and Miles Hutton and John Stanes went for Beetham using money collected from the parishioners.[165] Thinking that grievances about tithes were about to be redressed, the parishioners of Heversham witheld their great tithes which were due to the Abbey of St Mary, York.[166]

Any illusions that the Duke of Norfolk was waiting for conference at Richmond were quickly dispelled. A meeting was scheduled for Monday 5 February at the Greyfriars, but no gentlemen were present, and the citizens of Richmond would have nothing to do with the visitors.[167] Thus the last attempt of men of the Lake Counties to unite with the allies in Yorkshire failed.

By the end of January it was also evident that the Pilgrimage of Grace had failed. The Duke of Norfolk had virtually been given a free hand by the King on the assumption, as Norfolk put it, that you 'take in good part whatsoever promise I shall make unto the rebels for surely I shall observe no part thereof'.[168] On these conditions Henry was even willing to waive his previously adamant demands for the execution of ten ringleaders. When Norfolk met forty of the rebel leaders at White Friars in Doncaster on 6 December, he was therefore able to promise all that they requested. When Aske and the other Pilgrims went on their knees to beg for a pardon from the King, Norfolk was able to give it. As to their grievances, these were cleverly deferred by an agreement to call a northern parliament at which all the rebel articles could be discussed. No details of where or when the parliament would be held were given. The only concession which was made concerned the restoration of suppressed abbeys pending further discussion of their future at the parliament.

On 7 December Aske announced the terms of the peace to the waiting rebels. Some opposition was extinguished, and on the

[163]*Ibid.*, 959.
[164]*Ibid.*, 965.
[165]*Ibid.*, 671.
[166]*Ibid.*, 671(2), iii.
[167]Dodds, Vol. II, pp. 105-6.
[168]*LP,* XI, 864.

following day Lancaster Herald read the pardon and the rebels began to disperse. Aske relinquished his title of captain, and the badge of five wounds was ceremoniously disposed of.

Six weeks later no movement had been made towards the calling of a parliament, and the delaying tactics of the King were taking effect. On one hand interest and faith in the rebellion had been lost, and the cohesiveness of the rebels had degenerated into disunity. On the other hand, the extreme rebels who had no faith in the word of the King attempted to rekindle the insurrection, and they provided the King with the excuse to take the heads which he had denied himself by granting the pardon. One such excuse was provided by a rising in the East Riding of Yorkshire in January 1537 which was led by Sir Francis Bigod and John Hallam. Having no faith in the promises of the King they devised a plan to capture Hull and Scarborough. However, the rising was poorly prepared and degenerated into a fiasco. Only a few hundred rebels joined Bigod, and neither of their objectives was attained. Hallam was captured, and Bogod fled towards the north west.

The second excuse was provided by the men of the Lake Counties in February 1537.

February 1537

The outcome of the political line-up in the rebellion of 1536 was to enhance the reputation of the Earl of Cumberland for his loyalty and to cause speculation to the effect that Lord Dacre might have been behind the rebels.[169] In the light of this it is ironic that the second rising of 1537 disproved any such theories. The new rebellion was stimulated by an ill-conceived Clifford action, was to a large extent motivated by hatred of the Cliffords, and was dramatically destroyed by a Dacre.

At some time before January 1537 an order was sent out by the Duke of Norfolk instructing the loyal gentlemen of the region to apprehend the rebel leaders, including Nicholas Musgrave and Thomas Tebay. Thomas Clifford, the Earl of Cumberland's bastard son, made two attempts to arrest these men but was twice frustrated by the laws of sanctuary, for the fugitives were sheltered in the church steeple.[170] Clifford might have learned caution from the enclosure riots which followed the first attempt in early January, but on 12

[169]*Ibid.*, 1331.
[170]*Ibid.*, XII(1), 687(2).

February he returned with 'strong thieves of the Westlands' who began to spoil the town of Kirkby Stephen. The townspeople rose against the intruders and a battle ensued before Clifford retreated to the shelter of Brougham castle near Penrith. Having committed themselves to the new rebellion, the people sent out letters encouraging neighbouring areas to join the rising.[171]

A combination of motives can be identified for the new disturbance. Perhaps most important was the frustration of the rebels after weeks of waiting for the first tangible evidence of the success of the Pilgrimage of Grace. As time had passed the visions of impending concessions to rebel demands had disappeared, and euphoria was replaced by a growing anger at having been duped. Distrust of the government was reinforced by the move to arrest Musgrave and Tebay. The rebels may have heard of other arrests in Yorkshire and probably were aware of the imprisonment of Sir Francis Bigod at Carlisle Castle.[172] It is unlikely that the rebels wanted to make a dramatic bid to rescue Bigod, but the threat against their own leaders was enough to precipitate new action. An additional stimulus was the deep grievance, partly economic but mainly political, against the Cliffords. The weak wardenship, the Scots' threat, the refusal of Lord Clifford to surrender Carlisle, and the last straw of Thomas Clifford's raid demanded action.[173] It was therefore logical to make Carlisle the target. The only difference between this and the first attempt to take the city in October was that the new rising, born in violence, directed the fury of the commons towards using violence in return.

The urgency of the men of Kirkby Stephen was transmitted throughout the region, and near-panic can be detected in a letter which was relayed to sympathisers from Kendal.[174]

> at morn was un belapped on every side with our enemies the captain of Carlisle and gentlemen of our county of Westmorland, and hath destroyed and slain many our brethren and neighbours. Wherefore we desire your aid, according to your oaths, and this Tuesday we desire you to be at Kendal before eight o'clock or we are likely to be destroyed.

The gentlemen at Carlisle and the Duke of Norfolk in Yorkshire were aware that Carlisle was the rebel target, and Norfolk put the blame for the rising firmly on the shoulders of Thomas Clifford saying, 'and that

[171]*Ibid.*, 419.
[172]Dodds, Vol. II, p. 114.
[173]See above, pp. 28, 82-3.
[174]*LP*, XII(1), 411.

they had not spoiled, this had not happened'.[175] Fearing the consequences of a rebel success at Carlisle, Norfolk wrote to Sir Christopher Dacre.

> I will not instruct you what ye shall do, for ye know better than I. And spare not frankly to slay plenty of these false rebels to prove my old sayings that Sir Christopher Dacre is a true Knight to his sovereign lord, an hardy Knight, and a man of war. Pinch now no courtesy to shed blood of false traitors; and be ye busy on one side, and ye may be sure that the Duke of Norfolk will come on the other. Finally now, Sir Christopher, or never. Your loving cousin if ye do well now, or else enemy for ever.[176]

Despite Norfolk's veiled threat this letter must have carried more weight with Sir Christopher than the letters from Sir John Lowther, Thomas Clifford and a lesser gentleman, John Barnfield, in which the defenders of Carlisle commanded that 'ye with as many as ye trust come unto the King's castle in all goodly haste possible, for as we are informed the commons will be this day upon the Broadfield'.[177]

While such efforts were being made to organise the defence of Carlisle, Sir Thomas Wharton, Sir Thomas Curwen and others were sent into the Lake Counties to try to draw the rebels away from the city.[178] Their instructions were 'to set fire in many places of the rebels dwelling, thinking thereby to make them scale, and if the traitors so sparcle they shall not spare shedding of blood'.

This action appears to have been too late, or ineffective. On 17 February the commons advanced on the city. At the moment of the rebel assault, after the first discharge of arrows, Sir Christopher Dacre 'showed himself a trewe noble Knight by riding down on the rebels with this own force'.[179] This relieved the pressure on the city, and gave the besieged occupants the chance to issue forth and pursue the dispirited rebels.[180] Thomas Clifford was at the head of the

[175]*Ibid.*, 439.

[176]*Ibid.*, 419.

[177]*Ibid.*, 427.

[178]*Ibid.*, 419.

[179]*Ibid.*, 448.

[180]An unusual description of the siege at Carlisle can be found in Wilfred Holme, *The Fall and Evil Success of Rebellion, 1572* edited by H. Binneman:

> For at Carlyle they lost with shooting at the citie,
> As their arrowes their artillerie most principall,
> And then fled away from their villanous enormytie,
> This perceyved by the citie and gentlemen patrimoniall,
> They came forth with speares substantiall
> Well horsed in aray following in a chase,
> By whome they lost their crosse their standard principal,

pursuit and Norfolk mentioned that 'he had atoned for his former fault' by following the commons for twelve miles.[181] Norfolk believed that six or seven hundred of the rebels were taken. So it was that the rebellion in the Lake Counties ended.

Large numbers of rebels who had been captured awaited the arrival of the Duke of Norfolk and could only expect the ultimate punishment for the crime of treason. The rebels who escaped fled to the temporary shelter of their homes. The great lords of the region waited to see how their behaviour might affect the future power structure on the Western March. The Earl of Cumberland, though loyal, had failed to serve his King in any positive fashion, and he and his family had, albeit inadvertently, contributed to the outbreak of the first rising and directly triggered the second. Lord Dacre must have had considerable sympathy with the rebels, and no doubt saw in the rebellion an opportunity to strike back at the Cliffords and the crown. However, Dacre had escaped charges of treason by the skin of his teeth in the trial of 1534 and was in consequence apprehensive of involvement in the Pilgrimage of Grace. Should the rebellion fail, he could not hope for escape a second time. Therefore Lord Dacre had remained loyal but by leaving the area had failed to restrain his own tenants. His family and servants had acted dubiously in the first rising and only in a moment of crisis during the second had they used the power which was always at their disposal. With neither Clifford nor Dacre acquiring great honour from the events of the rebellion, the arrival of the Duke of Norfolk must also have caused them some trepidation.

Epilogue

It is not within the scope of this study to examine in detail the events of the latter part of 1537 or the long-term consequences of the Pilgrimage of Grace. However, three aspects of the aftermath of the rebellion demand scrutiny: the punishment meted out to the rebels; the precedent which the dissolution of Furness Abbey in 1537 set for all other larger monasteries in England and Wales; and the political changes which were made in the region in an attempt to strengthen the King's influence on the western march.

Norfolk arrived at Carlisle on Sunday, 20 February, and was the

> And had three hundred taken within a little space.
> The other fled away as shepe with wolves chased,
> Some oppressed, some spoiled, some with lamentation,
> Thus five thousand by five hundred were utterly defaced,
> Hunted like dogs for their abomination,
>   . . .!'

[181]*LP,* XII(1), 448.

first to acknowledge that the apportionment of blame would not be easy. In a letter to the King he indicated the problems which would be created if he proceeded to try the rebels by jury.

> And surely if I should have proceeded by the trial of twelve men I think not the fifth man of this should have suffered for the common saying is here I came out of fear of loss of all my goods and I came forth for fear of burning of my house and defacing of my wife and children. And a small excuse will be believed here where much affection and pity of neighbours doth reign.[182]

From the estimated six thousand offenders who had returned to Carlisle for pardon or judgement, seventy-four of the ringleaders were chosen and sentenced to death by martial law.[183] Worried that the King would not consider this to be a sufficient number Norfolk wrote, 'yet I think the like number hath not been heard of put to execution at any one time'.[184] In fact, the number caused a problem, for the scarcity of iron precluded the hanging of all seventy-four in chains.

While preparations for the executions were going on, Norfolk ordered the pursuit of those prominent men who had not been taken, and investigations began to discover the cause of the rising. As has been shown, the blame was variously apportioned between religious and economic motives.[185] Norfolk's opinion tended towards the latter, and he particularly identified high entry fines, increases in rents, and enclosures as prime reasons for rebellion. Evidently he had some sympathy with the economic complaints of the rebels, for he commented 'that they have been so sore handled in times past, which as I and all here think was the only cause of this rebellion'.[186]

Even so, an example was to be made of the traitors. Most of them were executed in their own villages, although two were taken to London to be questioned.[187] Several additions must be made to the list of seventy-four rebels condemned to die on 24 February.[188] A separate hearing occurred at Lancaster to try the canons and tenants involved in the commotion which had occurred at Cartmel after the pardon. Of the nine canons tried, four were found guilty and executed, three escaped, and two were acquitted. Sixteen husbandmen

[182]PRO, S.P.1, 116, pp. 108-11, (*LP*, XII(1), 498).

[183]*LP*, XII(1), 498. See Appendix II for names and places of origin of the 74 executed rebels.

[184]*Ibid*.

[185]*Ibid*., 478. See Introduction.

[186]*Ibid*., 478.

[187]These were Barnard Towneley and Robert Thompson.

[188]*LP*, XII(1), 498.

were also tried of whom ten were found guilty and hanged, three were acquitted and three escaped.[189] Several other rebels were tried separately. William Lancaster, parson of Beetham, was tried at Lancaster and hanged. [190] William Barret, the tanner from Craven who was present at the attack on Carlisle was tried at Manchester and hanged.[191] John Stanes, the rebel leader of Beetham was hanged in Westmorland.[192] John Atkinson was reported to have been captured, in which case he would certainly have been hanged.[193] Barnard Towneley was taken to London, was thoroughly questioned and executed there.[194]

The fate of the other prominent rebel leaders is unknown. Robert Thompson, the vicar of Brough, was taken to the Tower of London where he made comprehensive statements concerning his part in the rising. He was still alive and in the Tower in late 1537, at which time he wrote to Cromwell reaffirming his innocence after the declaration of the pardon. Had anything been proven against him he would certainly have been executed, but as evidence of this is lacking he must be presumed to have died in prison, Cromwell having rejected his appeal.[195] Of Nicholas Musgrave, Robert Pulleyn and William Collins nothing more is known. As all three were deeply involved in the second rising it must be presumed that they were amongst the number killed at Carlisle during the attack, or that they evaded capture. Even so, the total number executed after the rebellion was ninety-two or ninety-three for the Lake Counties as a whole. The spring brought with it the arrest and execution of more prominent rebels from Yorkshire and the north east. Sir Thomas Percy, Sir Francis Bigod and Lord Darcy were three of the rebel leaders who preceded Robert Aske to the scaffold. However, for the Pilgrimage of Grace as a whole the total number of sufferers was 178, and although individually the rebels in the Lake Counties were less notorious, the region provided a remarkably high proportion of the executed.[196]

[189]'Narrative of the Traitors of Whalley and Cartmel', *Chetham Miscellanies,* new ser., 90 (1931).

[190]*LP,* XII(1), 1104(8).

[191]*Ibid.,* 632.

[192]*Ibid.*

[193]*Ibid.,* 825.

[194]*Ibid.,* XII(2), 291(ii), which exempts him from the pardon.

[195]*Ibid.,* 1339.

[196]G.R. Elton, *Policy and Police. The Enforcement of the Reformation in the Age of Thomas Cromwell,* p. 387. Of this number 46 were executed for their part in the Lincolnshire rising.

The condemned rebels were not allowed to rest even after their execution. On 8 May the Duke of Norfolk wrote to Cromwell, denying that he had given permission for the bodies to be cut down from their gallows and buried.[197] That this new crime had been allowed to happen he blamed on the gentlemen of the region, and particularly the Earl of Cumberland. Having received severe criticism for permitting this course of events, Norfolk initiated a major investigation into the removal of bodies.[198] In a letter of 16 May he presented a report citing ten incidents in which corpses had been removed. Three cases concerned Cockermouth, two each at Braithwaite and Brigham, and others at Torpenhow, Dearham and Bridekirk.[199] The responsibility was attributed to the wives and mothers of the executed men, but the King demanded further investigation as he believed that the conspiracy 'could not have come only of women's heads'.[200] In the last surviving letter on the subject Cromwell was still demanding that Norfolk should 'find out and punish the principal doers'.[201] Thus it was that, from the viewpoint of the commons of the Lake Counties, the Pilgrimage of Grace came to a sorry and sordid end. The bodies of rebel leaders on gallows in many villages provided grim warning for any who still dared to challenge the authority of their King.

The Pilgrimage of Grace only served to delay the suppression of the smaller monasteries such as Conishead and Cartmel.[202] The threat to the larger institutions did not arise until the process of punishing the rebels had begun. Where, as in the case of Whalley, a monastery in the person of its abbot and brethren could be proved to have committed treason, it was seized as attainted land.[203] Such seizures were exceptional and did not provide the King and Cromwell with the precedent which they required for the dissolution of the other large monasteries. That precedent was provided by Furness Abbey.

It has been shown that during the course of the rebellion the Abbot of Furness made every attempt to ensure the continued existence of the monastery.[204] To this end he had ordered his brethren to fight

[197]*LP,* XII(1), 1156.

[198]*Ibid.,* 1156.

[199]*Ibid.,* 1214.

[200]*Ibid.,* 1257.

[201]*Ibid.*

[202]The possessions of Cartmel and Conishead were added to the Estates of the Duchy of Lancaster, Bouch and Jones, p. 55.

[203]*LP,* XII(1), 632.

[204]See above, p. 105. A full account of the events at Furness appears in Haigh. *Lancashire Monasteries,* Chapters VI and VII.

alongside the rebels while at the same time he fled to the Earl of Derby to assure him of the monastery's loyalty to the King. The King's pardon effectively wiped the slate clean for Furness, but thereafter the brethren of the Abbey provided the King with new evidence of treason. Prophecies were circulated concerning the death of the King, the supremacy in the Church was criticised, and the King's officers were reviled.[205] Abbot Pyle was deeply concerned that the expression of such sentiments could endanger the future of the abbey. He therefore tried to keep the treasonable talk quiet and to impose new and strict discipline on the monastery by enforcing the injunctions of Leyton and Legh which had previously been ignored.[206] The one pro-Henrician reformist amongst the brethren, Friar Legate, was intimidated by Abbot Pyle to stop him informing the King's officers of what had taken place.[207]

In April 1537 the Abbot was summoned to Whalley Abbey where the Earl of Sussex was investigating the causes of the rebellion in Lancashire. Before leaving the abbey Pyle called all his brethren to the chapter house and commanded them that 'they should not meddle with them [the King's officers] nor show anything at all to them, or else by Him that made him he should go to prison and never come out so long as he was Abbot'.[208]

However, the monastery was too divided within itself to be able to cover up all its crimes. Several of the monks were willing to give evidence out of loyalty to the King or a desire to save themselves. Despite these divisions only two of the monks, Henry Salley and John Broughton, were committed to jail and the whole monastery could not be seized as attainted land, something which evidently disappointed Sussex and Cromwell.[209]

The solution to their problem lay in the attitude of Abbot Pyle. Whereas he had always tried to save the monastery, he was also concerned to save his own skin. His flight to the Earl of Derby was not an entirely unselfish gesture to prove the loyalty of the Abbey to the King, for it was also a safe course to security.[210] By the time of the summons to Whalley Pyle appears to have been a very frightened man. No doubt he feared execution, the fate of his fellow Abbot Paslew of Whalley. An idea may have been present in his mind that he

[205]*LP,* XII(1), 841(3), i and ii.

[206]*Ibid.,* 841(4).

[207]*Ibid.,* 841(3).

[208]*Ibid..*

[209]*LP,* XII(1), 840.

[210]See above, p. 105.

had only two possible alternatives, the surrender of the abbey or of his own life. When Sussex suggested that as an act of loyalty, the abbey should be surrendered, Pyle willingly acceded. A document was written in which he acknowledged 'the misorder and evil lives, both unto God and our Prince, of the brethren of the said monastery', and in which he voluntarily surrendered Furness Abbey to the King.[211]

Having set the precedent that it was within the powers of the abbot to surrender an institution of which he was in only temporary control, other monasteries throughout the country were persuaded to follow suit.[212]

Holm Cultram, the only other large monastery to have played a significant part in the Pilgrimage of Grace in the Lake Counties, was to fall in this way. In May 1537 charges were made against the Abbot by one of the monks, Thomas Graham.[213] The most serious of the charges concerned the incitement of tenants and brethren to rebel, and speaking treasonable words.[214] As well as this the Abbot was alleged to have broken the King's Injunctions by bringing women to dine in the monastery, by selling off plate worth £100 and some jewels, by giving away some gold and silver plate, by letting out the demesne lands of the monastery and by using the abbey seal to the detriment of the King's profit. Graham's motives in bringing the charges are unmistakeable. On 10 August 1536 Abbot Thomas Ireby had died and Graham had offered the King four hundred marks over and above the first fruits if he gained the preferment of the abbacy.[215] However, Abbot Carter had been elected rather than Graham, possibly because of a disreputable incident in which the latter was moved from the office of proctor of Wigton Church because he had neglected his duty.[216] In the light of this it seems probable that Graham was getting his revenge on Carter by saying that 'all the insurrection there was owing to him'. Certainly Carter could not have hoped to escape the fate of the monks of Cartmel. However, he was never attainted and his disappearance from the records may be explained by natural death. In the event, the fate of Carter was irrelevant to the prospects of Holm Cultram. Gawyn Borrowdale

[211]*LP*, XII(1), 832.

[212]G.W.O. Woodward. *The Dissolution of the Monasteries* (London, 1966).

[213]*LP*, XII(1), 1259.

[214]*Ibid.*, 1259(3).

[215]*Ibid.*, XI, 276, 319.

[216]F. Grainger and W.G. Collingwood, *Register and Records of Holm Cultram* (Kendal, 1929), p. 154.

was made the last Abbot, and his duty was to surrender the abbey.[217]
Most of the great abbeys terminated their existence by surrender in
this fashion, and Furness had provided them with the example to
follow.

The immediate political effect of the Pilgrimage of Grace in the
Lake Counties was to expose the ineptitude of the Earl of Cumberland
as warden of the western march. Soon after the arrival in the region of
the Duke of Norfolk, the search started for a suitable successor.
Norfolk concisely summed up the situation.

> As to the west marches, though no man can serve the King better
> than Lord Dacre, yet as he was so late at the bar and paid a great
> fine it would not be expedient to put him thereunto, else men
> might say a quarrel was picked to him to get his money and that
> had, he was put again in office. I think Sir Thomas Wharton will
> never serve the King well as warden; so that my Lord of
> Cumberland is most meet, but he must be brought to change his
> conditions and not be so greedy to get money of his tenants.[218]

The Privy Council did not share Norfolk's opinion that 'a mean
person should not have the wardenship of the west marches, and that to
keep the wild people of all three marches in order will require men of
good estimation and nobility'.[219] Instead they suggested that 'The
King has been worse served on the west borders through the
controversy between great men there, and if he removed the Earl of
Cumberland and prefer the Lord Dacre the 'pyke' between them will
only be increased; on the other hand, if he appoint the meanest man to
rule there, is not his Grace's authority sufficient to make him
respected?'[220] The Duke of Norfolk reaffirmed his opinion that only
Clifford or Dacre were suitable,[221] to which the King angrily
rejoined that 'we will not be bound to accept the service of none but
lords'.[222] He had decided that Wharton should in future be his
representative on the border, and consequently requested that the
Earl of Cumberland resign his wardenship. The Earl was advanced to
the Order of the Garter in April 1537, presumably in recognition of

---

[217]*Ibid.*, pp. 55-6.

[218]*LP,* XII(1), 594. An alternative interpretation of the political consequences of the
rebellion appears in M.L. Bush, 'The Problem of the Far North', *Northern History* 6
(1971).

[219]*Ibid.*

[220]*Ibid.*, XII(1), 636.

[221]*Ibid.*, 919.

[222]*Ibid.*, 1118.

his loyal service during the Pilgrimage of Grace, and in response to the King's letter informing him of the changed situation wrote that he 'will always be ready to follow His Highness' pleasure'.[223] In June Wharton was made Deputy Warden of the march, for which office he received two hundred marks and the fruits of perquisites normally associated with the wardenship.[224] By 1544 he was earning six hundred marks annually, having been made Thomas Lord Wharton and full warden. This would suggest that the King had succeeded in establishing a new man in power on the border. In September 1537 Wharton wrote to Cromwell saying that 'In the late Lord Dacre's day there was a cry "A Dacre, a Dacre". Now only "A King, a King" '[225] In fact Wharton's optimism was short lived. The Cliffords resented him and gave his wardenship little active support, and the Dacres saw no good reason to change their old attitude towards him. Thus in 1538 Wharton reported that 'neither of both the said Lords loveth me' and voiced criticism of their lack of cooperation.[226] The old order could not be replaced at a stroke, and Lord Dacre was to return to power before the reign of Henry VIII had expired. However, in the short-term the appointment of Wharton was a most bitter blow to the men of the Lake Counties. Their call for the return of the old order as personified by Lord Dacre was unanswered, and instead Thomas Wharton, one of the new men campaigned against by the Pilgrims and a man particularly disliked in his own region, became the King's representative on the border.

[223]*Ibid.*, 373.

[224]See James, 'Change and Continuity', and Bush, 'Problem of The Far North'.

[225]*LP*, XII(2), 642.

[226]*Ibid.*, 422.

CONCLUSION

Three questions remain to be answered: what was the balance of motives of the rebels in the Lake Counties; what contribution did the rebellion there make towards the Pilgrimage of Grace; and where does the rebellion in the Lake Counties stand within the context of Tudor history and in relation to other medieval and early modern popular movements?

The generally accepted view of the Pilgrimage of Grace in the Lake Counties has been that rebellion was motivated by economic stress, class hatred and anti-clericalism.[1] None of these assumptions has any genuine foundation. The rebellion there has been misrepresented, usually by reference to the more dramatic statements of an individual or minority group which do not represent the spirit of the whole rising.

Before attempting broader generalisations about this local rebellion the point must be made that variations of motive, behaviour and objective were present throughout this large region. Undoubtedly the men of Cumberland were less interested in spiritual matters than those of Westmorland; at the same time they were more concerned with the preservation of stability on the border. Allowing for such variations, generalisations can nevertheless be made about the rising in the Lake Counties as a whole.

It is no doubt true that there would have been no great disturbances had the commons of the Lake Counties not been faced by considerable economic pressures. For the first time enclosures were being seen as an evil, disturbing traditional rights and enabling great lords to parcel up land and let it out on terms which, in comparison with customary tenures, were extremely severe. This was especially the case with entry fines and gressums which were being enhanced on the properties of long-serving tenant families as well as on those of new occupiers. When harvest failure and shortage were added to the burden of the peasantry of the region, disturbances were likely. Riots occurred in 1535, and even without the Pilgrimage of Grace in Lincolnshire and Yorkshire would have occurred in 1536 too.

However, economic factors alone are insufficient to explain the scale and purpose of the rebellion. Nor can the conflict which undoubtedly did occur between landlord and tenant be written off as a manifestation of class hatred. The commons of the Lake Counties pursued an essentially rational course in their rebellion and did not

[1] See Introduction.

intend to 'put an end to gentlemen'.[2] In fact, their course was reactionary rather than radical. A great deal of time was spent in peacefully persuading gentlemen to put their seals to documents which bound both parties to adhere to tradition. Threats of violence were used, even against the more respected gentlemen such as Sir James Layburn of Kendal. But as was shown in his case the execution of such threats was deferred until other alternatives had been explored.[3] Once the agreement of gentlemen to custom had been assured, even the most unpopular considered themselves safe. In the case of Sir William Musgrave, the taking of the rebel oath, and presumably adherence to rebel demands, was enough to ensure a free passage through rebel territory.[4] The reason for this is mainly that such gentlemen had no further part to play in a rebellion which was being led, organised, and executed by the peasantry. No doubt the rebel leaders welcomed Sir Edward Musgrave's voluntary surrender and would have appreciated the influence of Sir John Lowther on their behalf at the negotiations with Carlisle. However, gentlemen such as these were dispensable once their adherence was gained and did not henceforth feature prominently in the rebels' plans. The only real evidence of a tenant's hatred of his landlord occurs in particular cases. Evidence of the rapacity of the Earl of Cumberland, Sir Thomas Wharton, Peter Middleton, John Legh and others is substantial enough to show that the tenants of these men, who no doubt were primarily motivated by economic pressures, rebelled with good reason. These tenants were a minority of a larger movement — one which shared their views, but not to the exclusion of other motives.

In mentioning the positions of gentlemen, one must not exclude political undercurrents which were present throughout the time of the disturbance. The contribution of nobles and their factions was a negative though important one: feuding between the Cliffords and Dacres had the effect of neutralising the forces of law and order, thus allowing the commons, if only for a few months, to fill the power vacuum.[5] On the other hand, there were also positive factors. Sir Thomas Wharton and the Cliffords were not only detested because of their economic policies. The loyal tenants and servants of the Dacres were willing to pursue their lord's cause against rivals, even without a specific command to do so. Wharton did well to hide himself during the months of rebellion: he had as much to fear from the tenants of

[2]*LP*, XII(1), 687(1); Tawney, *Agrarian Problem*, p. 319.

[3]See above, p. 108.

[4]See above, p.110.

[5]See above, p. 38.

the Dacres as from his own, and this fact was founded in the political climate which had developed in the region during past decades.

What is suggested here is that many of the commons, far from rebelling against their lords, were trying to retain both the traditional economic links and the almost feudal relationship which existed between border tenant and lord. Far from being a class-war, certain elements of the rebellion demonstrate the continued existence of the ideal of a bond between rulers and servants which had long since snapped elsewhere. The reason for the continuation of the feudal relationship is not hard to find: the answer lies with the continually disturbed border situation.[6] The commons knew well the threat to their livelihood which was evident at times of weakness on the western march. Dacre tenants were not alone in feeling that a Clifford offered little protection against the ravages of the Scots. Whether Lord Dacre liked it or not, the commons of the Lake Counties had a strong political motive which was based upon loyalty to his house. The peasant who voiced the much-quoted sentiment against gentlemen leaders was thus also one of a minority.[7] Despite him, other rebels went with Sir John Lowther to conduct the business of the deputy warden of the march. For the peasants, Lowther's efforts to maintain the security of the border were better than none at all. It was not against him that charges of incompetence were levelled by the commons, but against his commander, the Earl of Cumberland.

Writers have suggested that the rebels of the Lake Counties had no leaders. The fact that they were able to elect their own commanders belies such an idea. In fact, it was not the peasants who were leaderless, but the gentlemen. With the exception of one or two, such as Sir Thomas Curwen, the gentlemen of the region were forced either to flee the rebels, or to adhere to their demands and subsequently to follow along behind the musters in positions of insignificance. The fact that this was the case suggests two things about the relationship between peasants and gentlemen in the region. The first is that, having sworn gentlemen to observe their custom, the rebels had achieved one aim and were now going on towards other objectives which lay beyond economics. The second is that the peasants, being thwarted by the absence of the accepted leaders of their feudal society, were nevertheless willing to pursue an essentially feudal style of rebellion on their own initiative. In other words, while no gentlemen were willing to be taken as leaders, and while there was great hostility expressed towards some, such as the Earl of Cumberland, had a Dacre come

[6] See above, p. 28.
[7] *LP*, XII(1), 687(2).

forward to lead the rebellion he would have been welcomed. Had this been the case the rebellion would have assumed new proportions. Certainly Carlisle, which contained many citizens loyal to Dacre influence, could have fallen. Then a powerful and well organised rebel army with much greater unity than any in Yorkshire would have been ready to turn its attention southwards.

Economic motives were thus fundamental to the rising. Political motives were also present and of considerable significance. But what of religion? In this aspect of the rebellion the peasants of the Lake Counties have been severely criticized as being anti-clerical and unconcerned with the issues raised by the Henrician Reformation. It is possible to cite Percy Simpson's statement that all would not be well until the heads of priests were stricken off, but it must be asked whether his sentiments were typical.[8] The evidence shows that they were not. With the exception of the southwest of the region the rebels had little sympathy with the monasteries, but these institutions were not common in the Lake Counties, and those which did exist had a severely tainted reputation. However, the rebels were greatly disturbed by the rumours circulating in the north concerning the future of their churches, church goods, and services.[9] Furthermore they were upset about the tangible changes taking place in the everyday practice of traditional Catholic ritual. The fact that they did not understand the Ten Articles, the liturgical debates of the early Reformation, or the motives of their King is hardly relevant. In general they were simple people with simple spiritual needs, and it would be cynical to say that the rebel oath, the 'Captains Mass' and the compulsory preaching at musters represented anything less than genuine devotion.[10] Evidence of anti-clericalism is in fact generally meagre. Certainly raids on tithe barns cannot be regarded as examples of anti-clericalism, for the barns which were broken into were the property of unpopular lay tithe-farmers. Official rebel policy on tithes was constructive, and criticism, such as that of the Abbey of St Mary's at York, selective.[11] Similarly, attacks on clerics were not widespread and fall into two groups: attacks on pluralists, who featured specifically in the rebels' demands for reform; and attacks on priests who refused to keep the traditional ways of the old Church. The religious feelings of the peasantry of the Lake Counties may have had little in common with

[8]*Ibid.*

[9]See above, pp. 72-3.

[10]Dickens, 'Secular and Religious Motivation', pp. 50-1 provides a contrary interpretation.

[11]See above, p. 59.

those of Robert Aske, but religious feelings there certainly were. The factor which precipitated the region into rebellion, which bound the rebels together, and which gave them a just cause in which they could believe, was religion. It interacted with political and economic grievances, and together they prompted a movement of massive solidarity. Without the presence of any one of these motives the Pilgrimage of Grace in the Lake Counties would have been reduced to a series of minor stirrings. The combination of them all made the movement as determined and united as any other area of rebellion in 1536.

At this point one must consider the second question. Can the north-west be treated in isolation from other areas of rebellion, or was it part and parcel of the Pilgrimage of Grace? The custom amongst historians of the subject has been to segment the rising into three, four, or five parts.[12] Certainly this must be done, for individual regions behaved differently. However, considering the large area involved in the rising and the state of communications in the month of October in the sixteenth century, it seems strange that no one has commented on the singularity of purpose of the men of northern England. In fact, a strong case can be made to link Cumberland and Westmorland with other areas of rebellion. Perhaps most important, the rising would never have taken the shape it did if the men of Yorkshire had not urged their neighbours across the Pennines to rise.[13] The initial Yorkshire manifesto, read at Kendal, Kirkby Stephen, and Penrith, was thenceforth the backbone of the rebel programme in the Lake Counties. Inevitably, the behaviour of the rebels there was determined by their own particular situation and, as happened in other areas of rebellion, local complaints were added to the basic programme.

It has been said that the rebels in the north-west were a 'considerable anxiety to the leaders of the rebellion'.[14] This is not surprising when one considers the expectations of those leaders. They had nominated prominent gentlemen of the Lake Counties to attend their assembly, and only two of the less notable of these turned up, plus the genuine representatives of the commons' musters.

[12]For example, Dickens, 'Secular and Religious Motivation', and Davies, 'Pilgrimage of Grace Reconsidered'.

[13]See above, p. 91.

[14]See above, p. 2.

Anxiety would have appeared on two counts: that the rebels were not controlled by gentlemen in the manner of risings elsewhere, and that the leaders of this peasant rising were vociferous and enthusiastic. Indeed, these representatives maintained close communications with the rebels in Yorkshire and were able to persuade the gentlemen there to add the grievances of the Lake Counties to those of other areas of rebellion. The gentlemen's anxiety was proven well founded after the truce, for the rebellion in the Lake Counties maintained an impetus long after the enthusiasm had died elsewhere. The ultimate expression of this was the attack on Carlisle in February 1537. The men who then marched on Carlisle were by and large the same men who had followed the banner of the five wounds in 1536, and those executed in the aftermath of the second rising were hanged just as much for their part in the first. The high death toll of rebels in the Lake Counties is a genuine illustration of the extent to which the region contributed to the Pilgrimage of Grace as a whole.

Finally, what contribution does the rebellion in the Lake Counties make towards locating the Pilgrimage of Grace in historical perspective? In the conflict between differing interpretations of the rebellion the events of the Lake Counties are of considerable significance because the rising there has been seen to contain a large element of class-conflict.[15] This study could not agree with such an interpretation, for in most aspects the rebellion was a traditionalist one. This is surprising when one considers the popular characteristics of the rising in its leadership and organisation. Yet when one remembers that this was no anarchist rabble, but an alliance of the diverse classes of peasantry of the region to redress grievances against modernising trends in religion, politics and the economy, the rebels must be seen as trying to take a moderate step backwards rather than a revolutionary step forwards. This being the case, the Pilgrimage of Grace as a whole can no longer be seen as it has been portrayed in the past. The men of Cumberland and Westmorland were not the advance guard of class warfare, bound by an uneasy alliance to representatives of the old order such as Lord Darcy. Having forced the gentlemen of their own region to abide by the dictates of tradition, the commons of the Lake Counties were able to set about finding solutions to their other problems — to secure their economic position, to re-establish the old political order which was vital for their protection, and to preserve the religious traditions to which they were accustomed. In the Tudor age, when the strength of the monarchy was one of the few unchanging elements, all of these causes, like all the Pilgrimage of Grace, were doomed to failure.

[15]The view of Tawney, *Agrarian Problem,* p. 319, and Reid, *The King's Council in the North,* p. 126.

APPENDICES

I. THE PETITION OF THE WESTMORLAND REBELS

Ryght honorable lord Darsey in our most humbly wysse plesed your lordchep to be advertysed that all we the comonnallytey of Westmorland ar in a dedemer to doo your sirvyce accordynge to your tenor and comandment at all tymes. Wherfore it wold pleasse your good lordchep appon your nobles to schew favor unto us consirnynge the welthe of our cutreythe and the proffett of the comanaltye the qwyche we thynke is the best for us be your better advise qwherin is all owre trest that is to say consirnynge the gyrsumes for power men to be layd aparte but only penny farm penny gyrsum with all the tythes to remayn to every man hys owne doynge therfor accordynge to their dewtye. Also taxes casten emongst the benefest men as well tham in abett with us as tham that was nott incument for the comenwelth wich we dyssyre of your lordchep to brawth your plesur thairin qwatt we may doo in all these causes for we thynke in our oppyneons that we may putt in thair rowmes to serve God oders that wald be glad to keep hospytallyte for sum of thaim are no preests that hath the benefyce in hand and oders of thaim is my lord Crumwell chapplyns. Now as we doo accepte no gentyllman of our conseyll becawsse we be affrayed of thaim as and all to haffe nowt gyelt and sargeant corne layd down quiyche we thynke was great welthe forall the cutrethe and all that intaks ar noysum for power men to be layd down for all thes premysses aforesayd we besuche your noble lordchep of your goodnes and dyscreet consell wat may doo in the sayd premysses for the comen welthe to haffe knowlege in wryten by yur berer for we haff more trest in your lordchep then in any other and so we schall dayly prey to god to hayre from your good lordchep to gods plesur and your harts dyssyre from Kyrkby Stephyn the XVIIII day of November.

By your servant Robert Pullen and Nycolls Musgyffe the captayns of Westmorland and the comanallyte of the saym.

II. REBELS EXECUTED IN WESTMORLAND AND CUMBERLAND

WESTMORLAND

St. Lawrence's Appleby	Hugh Nutt, Richard Burrell, George Morland.
St. Michael's Appleby	William Nelson, Rowland Raysebeck, John Hall, Hugh Beyle, Robert Hodgeson, William Waterman, Launcelot Dragley, Hugh Stedeman.
Assheby	Edmund Sponer, John Smyth.
Bongate	Thomas Jackson.
Burgh	Christopher Blenkensoppe.
Dutton	John Dobson.
Hynganlownd (Hanginglands)	William Shawe, Hugh Dent, Lancelot Shaw, Edward Bowsfell, Richard Wallor, John Bowsfell, Roger Gibson, Jenkyn Wallor, John Rakestrawe.
Hurteley	Thomas Hall, William Wallour.
King's Meburne	John Bryan.
Kirkby Stephen	Thomas Tibee, Robert Rowlandeson, Edmund Playce, Peter Johnson, Thomas Syll.
Little Musgrave	Thomas Sutton, Anthony Emontson.
Mallerstang	Henry Gibson.
Nateby	Anthony Wharton.
Newhall	Thomas Westale, William Hodgeson, John Wylson, Anthony Tayllour, John Spencer.
Smardale	Gilbert Denyson.
Soreby	William Wylkyne, Thomas Taylour, Thomas Westale, Nynian Wallour.
Staynemore	Robert Patrick, Henry Gibson.
Sulby	Thomas Wrey, Henry Bursy.
Winton	Robert Smythe, Henry Bowsfell.

CUMBERLAND

Branthwayte	Christopher Smyth.
Brygham	John Wylson.
Cockermouth	Robert Fyssher, Thomas Bell.
Dereham	John Bewley.
Eglesfyld	Richard Cragge.
Emelton	John Jackeson.
Grastocke	William Buntyng.
Newton	Robert Goodale, Lancelot Richardson.
Penrith	Thomas Burtbecke, Edward Whitelocke, John Stephenson, Robert Stephenson, Michael Grey, William Stephenson, Sir Edward Penrith (chaplain), Edward Stephenson.
Perdishewe	Percival Hudson.
Talentyre	John Peyrson.
Wedoppe	Sander Banke.

Source:

PRO, S.P.1., 116, (*LP*, XII(1) 498).

BIBLIOGRAPHY

1. Primary Sources in Print

M. Bateson, 'The Pilgrimage of Grace and Aske's Examination', *EHR* 5, (1890)

J.S. Brewer, J. Gairdner, and R.H. Brodie (editors), *Letters and Papers, Foreign and Domestic, of the Reign of Henry VIII*, 23 vols. in 36 (London, 1862-1932)

A.G. Dickens, *Clifford Letters of the Sixteenth Century*, Surtees Society, vol. 172 (1962)

H. Ellis, *Original Letters Illustrative of English History*, 3, vol. II

W. Farrer, *Records Relating to the Barony of Kendale*, ed. John F. Curwen, 3 vols., (Kendal, 1923-6)

C. Fiennes, *The Journeys of Celia Fienes*, ed. Christopher Morris (London, 1949)

H. Fishwick, ed., *Pleadings and Depositions in the Duchy Court of Lancaster*, Lancashire and Cheshire Record Society, vols. 32-5 (1896-7)

H. Gee and W.J. Hardy, *Documents illustrative of English Church History* (London, 1896)

E. Hall, *The Triumphant Reigne of Kyng Henry VIII*, 2 vols., ed. Charles Whibley (London, 1904)

C. Hardwick, *A History of the Articles of Religion* (London, 1888)

W. Holme, *The Fall and Evill Successe of Rebellion, 1572*, ed. H. Binneman

J. Leland, *The Itinerary of John Leland in or about the Years 1535-43*, ed. L.T. Smith, 5 vols. (London, 1907-10)

'Narrative of the Indictment of Traitors of Whalley and Cartmel' in *Chetham Miscellanies*, XC, 1931

W. Ragg, 'The Foeffees of the Cliffords from 1283 to 1482', *Transactions of the Cumberland and Westmorland Antiquarian and Archaeological Society*, New Series 13 (1908)

T.N. Toller, *Correspondence of Edward, Third Earl of Derby*, Chetham Society, New Series 19 (1890)

Valor Eccesiasticus Tempore Henrici Octavus Institutus, ed., Caley and Hunter, 5 vols. (London, 1825)

2. Books

J.M.W. Bean, *The Estates of the Percy Family, 1416-1573* (Oxford, 1958)

C.M.L. Bouch and G.P. Jones, *An Economic and Social History of the Lake Counties, 1500-1830* (Manchester, 1961)

M. Bowker, *The Secular Clergy in the Diocese of Lincoln* (Cambridge, 1968)

B. Burke, *Dormant, Abeyant, Forfeited, and Extinct Peerages of the British Empire* (London, 1883)

D. Horton-Davies, *Worship and Theology in England. From Cranmer to Hooker, 1534-1603* (London, 1970), volume I of IV

A.G. Dickens, *The English Reformation* (London, 1964)

M.H. and R. Dodds, *The Pilgrimage of Grace 1536-7 and the Exeter Conspiracy 1538,* 2 vols (London, 1915)

G.R. Elton, *Policy and Police. The Enforcement of the Reformation in the Age of Thomas Cromwell* (London, 1972)
Reform and Reformation (London, 1977)
Star Chamber Stories (London, 1958)

A. Fletcher, *Tudor Rebellions* (London, 1968)

G. Grainger and W.G. Collingwood, *Registers and Records of Holm Cultram* (Kendal, 1929)

C. Haigh, *The Last Days of the Lancashire Monasteries and the Pilgrimage of Grace.* Chetham Society, third series, 7 (Manchester, 1969)
Reformation and Resistance in Tudor Lancashire (Cambridge, 1975)

P. Heath, *The English Parish Clergy on the Eve of the Reformation* (London, 1969)

C. Hill, *Economic Problems of the Church* (London, 1956)

J. Nicolson and R. Burn, *The History and Antiquities of the Counties of Westmorland and Cumberland,* 2 vols. (London, 1777)

F. Pollock and T.W. Maitland, *History of English Law before the Time of Edward the First,* 2 vols. (second edition, London, 1911)

T.I. Rae, *The Administration of the Scottish Frontier, 1513-60* (Edinburgh, 1966)

R.R. Reid, *The King's Council in the North* (London, 1921)

W. Rollinson, *A History of Man in the Lake District* (London, 1967)

A. Savine, *English Monasteries on the Eve of the Dissolution,* Oxford Studies in Social and Legal History 1 (1909)

R.B. Smith, *Land and Politics in the England of Henry VIII. The West Riding of Yorkshire, 1530-46* (Oxford, 1970)

R.L. Storey, *The End of the House of Lancaster* (London, 1966)

R.H. Tawney, *The Agrarian Problem in the Sixteenth Century* (London, 1912)

J. Thirsk, ed., *The Agrarian History of England and Wales*, vol. IV (London, 1967)

K. Thomas, *Religion and the Decline of Magic* (London, 1971)

D.L.W. Tough, *The Last Years of a Frontier. A History of the Borders during the Reign of Elizabeth* (Oxford, 1928)

· J. Whiteside, *Shap in Bygone Days* (Kendal, 1904)

J. Wilson, ed., *The Victoria History of England: Cumberland*, 2 vols. (London, 1905)

J. Wilson, *The Monasteries in Cumberland and Westmorland before the Dissolution* (Kendal, 1899)

G.W.O. Woodward, *The Dissolution of the Monasteries* (London, 1966)

3. Articles and Papers

M.L. Armitt, 'Fullers and Freeholders in the Parish of Grasmere', *Transactions of the Cumberland and Westmorland Antiquarian and Archaeological Society* (hereafter *CWAAS*) new series 8 (1908)

S.T. Bindoff, *Ket's Rebellion, 1549.* Historical Association, 1949

M. Bowker, 'Lincolnshire 1536: Heresy, Schism or Religious Discontent?' in D. Baker (ed.), *Studies in Church History,* 9 (9172)

M.L. Bush, 'The Problem of the Far North; a Study of the Crisis of 1537 and its consequences', *Northern History* 6 (9171)

W. Butler, 'Customs and Tenant Right Tenures of the Northern Counties', *CWAAS,* new series 26 (1926)

J. Cornwall, 'English County Towns in the 1520's, *Economic History Review,* 2nd series 17 (1965)

J. Cornwall, 'English Population in the Early Sixteenth Century', *Economic History Review,* 2nd series 23 (1970)

C.S.L. Davies, 'The Pilgrimage of Grace Reconsidered', *Past and Present* No. 41 (1968)

A.G. Dickens, 'Secular and Religious Motivation in the Pilgrimage of Grace', in G.J. Cuming (ed.) *Studies in Church History* 6 (1967)

G. Elliot, 'The System of Cultivation and Evidence of Enclosure in the Cumberland Open Fields, in the Sixteenth Century', *CWAAS,* new series 9 (1959)

T.H.B. Graham, 'Cornage and Drengage', *CWAAS,* new series 28 (1928)

F. Grainger, 'Agriculture in Cumberland in Ancient Times', *CWAAS,* new series 9 (1909)

W.G. Hoskins, 'Harvest Fluctuations and English Economic History 1480-1619', *Agricultural History Review* 12 (1964)

M.E. James, *Change and Continuity in the Tudor North. The Rise of Thomas First Lord Wharton,* University of York, Borthwick Papers, No. 27 (1965)

M.E. James, 'The First Earl of Cumberland (1493-1542) and the Decline of Northern Feudalism', *Northern History* 1 (1966)

M.E. James, 'Obedience and Dissent in Henrician England: The Lincolnshire Rebellion, 1536', *Past and Present* No. 48 (1970)

M.E. James, 'The Concept of Order and the Northern Rising', *Past and Present* No. 60 (1973)

J.E.A. Jolliffe, 'Northumbrian Institutions', *English Historical Review* 1926

B.C. Jones, 'Westmorland Pack-horse Men in Southampton', *CWAAS,* new series 59 (1959)

R.P. Littledale, 'Ennerdale', *CWAAS*, new series 31 (1931)

R.B. Outhwaite, *Inflation in Tudor and Early Stuart England,* Studies in Economic History, ed. M.W. Flinn (London, 1969)

D.M. Palliser, *The Reformation in York 1534-53,* University of York, Borthwick Papers, No. 40 (1971)

E.H. Phelps-Brown and S.V. Hopkins, 'Wage Rates and Prices, Evidence for Population Pressure in the Sixteenth Century', *Economica* 24 (1957)

J. Thirsk, 'Industries in the Countryside', F.J. Fisher (ed.) *Essays in Social and Economic History of Tudor and Stuart England,* 1961

4. Unpublished dissertations

S.E. Cott, 'The Career of Thomas Dacre, Second Lord Dacre, as Warden of the Scottish Marches', University of Manchester 1964

T.C.F. Darley, 'The Agrarian Economy of Westmorland', University of Leicester, 1965

G. Elliot, 'Aspects of the Development of the Agricultural Landscape in Cumberland', University of Liverpool, 1956

G. Jackson, 'The Wardenship of William Lord Dacre', University of Manchester, 1972

P. McNiven, 'Rebellion and Disaffection in the North of England 1403-8', University of Manchester, 1967

J.D.B. Sheail, 'The Regional Distribution of Wealth in England as indicated in the 1524-5 Lay Subsidy Returns', University of London, 1968

R.T. Spence, 'The Cliffords, Earls of Cumberland 1579-1646', University of London, 1959

INDEX

Other volumes in this series

Copies obtainable on order from
Swift Printers (Sales) Ltd., 1-7 Albion Place, Britton Street, London EC1M 5RE